ADVANCED RUNNING

TRAINING FOR BOTH SPORT AND COMPETITION, INCLUDING INDIVIDUAL RUNNING PLANS, ADVANCED SCHEDULES AND EXPERT ADVICE, SHOWN IN OVER 280 PHOTOGRAPHS

ELIZABETH HUFTON

southwater

This edition is published by Southwater, an imprint of Anness Publishing Ltd, Blaby Road, Wigston, Leicestershire LE18 4SE
email: info@anness.com
web: www.southwaterbooks.com; www.annesspublishing.com

Publisher: Joanna Lorenz
Project Editor: Amy Christian and Joanne Rippin
Photographers: Phil O'Connor and Mike King
Designer: Nigel Partridge
Production Controller: Bessie Bai

ETHICAL TRADING POLICY

Previously published as part of a larger volume, *The Complete Practical Encyclopedia of Running*

PICTURE CREDITS AND ACKNOWLEDGEMENTS
2:09 events: 70t, 77tl, 83br. Across the Divide (www.adventure-racing.org): 106t, 109t. Bridgeman Art Library: /Musee Municipal Antoine Vivenel, Compiegne, France, Lauros/ Giraudon: 8b. Corbis: /Bettmann: 9t, 10t, 11tr, 11b, 13tl, 13b, 53tr, 64t, 118t, /Fabrizio Bensch/ Reuters: 68b, /S. Carmona: 52t, /Duomo: 13tr, 41t, /Rick Friedman: 118b, /Li Ga/ Xinhua Press: 53b, /Gary Hershorn/ Reuters: 44t, /Karl-Josef Hildenbrand/ dpa: 31, /TempSport: 44b, /Gilbert Iundt/TempSport: 38t, /ALFRED CHEN JIN/ Reuters: 121tr, 121b, /Mike King: 42t, 42b, /Justin Lane/epa: 82b, /Wally McNamee: 49b, /Kerim Okten/epa: 45, /Neal Preston: 54b, /Franck Robichon/epa: 94, /Sampics/:48, /Stapleton Collection: 9b, /René Shenouda: 82t, /Roberto Tedeschi/epa: 95br, /Underwood & Underwood: 10b, /SUSANA VERA/ Reuters: 40, /Li Yue/xh/ Xinhua Press: 38b, /How Hwee Young/ epa: 41b, /Jeff Zelevansky/epa: 70b. Detail Events: 102 (all), 103 (all). Getty Images: /Allsport Hulton/Archive: 12t, /Allsport UK/Allsport: 124t, 124b, /PIERRE ANDRIEU/AFP: 123t, 123b, /Daniel Berehulak: 120b, /Julian Finney: 49t, 93t, /Stu Forster: 47br, /Gallo Images: 125t,/John Gichigi: 11b, /Paul Gilham: 47bl, /IOC Olympic Museum/ Allsport: 11tl, /Ross Kinnaird/Allsport: 39, /Leonard Mccombe/ Time Life Pictures:12b, /Chris McGrath/ ALLSPORT: 120t, /STAFF/AFP: 47t, /Michael Steele: 8t, /Touchline Photo/ALLSPORT: 125b, /PIERRE VERDY/ AFP/ Getty Images: 122t, 122b. Pete Hartley: 90t, 96, 97, 98t,98b, 99b, 100b, 101t, 104t, 104br, 105t, 105b, 116b. HoodtoCoast.com: 117t, 117b. Elizabeth Hufton: 116t. iStockphoto: 20b, 23b, 34bl, 60bl, 62b, 77tr, 108, 109b, 121tl. Philip O'Connor: 14, 15b, 16, 19t, 19b 20t, 24 (all), 25 (all), 26 (all), 27 (all), 28, 29 (all), 34t, 34bc, 34br, 35 (all), 36 (all), 37 (all), 46, 50, 55t, 60t, 61b, 64bl, 65, 67br, 68t, 72t, 72b, 74, 76, 77b, 80t, 80b, 81, 84 (all), 85bl, 85bc, 85br, 86t, 87tc, 87tl (x 2), 88b, 89, 92b, 93b, 99l. Mike King: 17t, 17b, 18b, 21 (all), 22 (all), 23tl, 23tc, 23tr, 30, 32 (all), 33 (all), 43 (all), 60br, 64br, 82t, 86b, 87tr, 91br, 92tr, 104bl. Runner's World Magazine: 7, 18t, 51, 61t, 67t, 74b, 75, 78, 78t, 78bl, 78br, 83t, 83bl, 85t, 87b, 88t, 90b, 91t, 91bl, 92tl, 95bl, 99tr, 100t, 101b, 106b, 107, 110 (all), 111 (all), 112 (all), 113 (all), 114t, 119 (all).

Models: Emily Crompton, Michael Egbor, Jo Freeman, Christophe Fromont, Chanelle Garnett, Suzi Hall (www.innovatefitness.com), Elizabeth Hufton, Sharon Knight, Mark Leary, Catherine Lee, Cressida Lorenz, Freddie Lorenz, David McCombes, Sophie Meer, Amber Milligan, Andrew Milligan, Jay Milligan, Russ Peake, Rebecca Rideout, Jessica Rideout, Oliver Stafford.

Thanks to Greenwich Leisure Ltd (GLL) for photography locations.

The author would like to thank: Keith Anderson, Mike Gratton, Suzi Hall, Steven Seaton and Steve Smythe for their expertise; Rupert Elkington-Cole for picture research; Brooks for kit; and Karen, Sarah, Helen, her family, and the staff of Runner's World magazine (UK).

CONTENTS

Introduction

People start running for many reasons. Some take it up to lose weight, get fit quickly, or to raise money for charity. Some are encouraged to run as children and never lose that habit. Some start running to improve their fitness for another sport. But whatever your reason for beginning to run in the first place, if you keep doing it for long enough, there will come a time when you feel the need to go a bit further.

For many runners that need is fulfilled by racing and that's when things really get serious. Nothing beats the feeling of reaching a start line and pinning on a number, the buzz of anticipation as you wonder whether months of dedication and hard training will pay off and the sheer rush of joy as you sprint over the finish line. You don't have to win a race to feel that you have something to prove; the number that is frozen on your watch is the benchmark you will fight to beat a few months down the line.

Once you've made the step up to competitive running you may find you become curious about different types of running. That could mean you want to go further, try an ultramarathon perhaps, or you decide to run in extreme conditions in another part of the world. You might be inspired to hit the track with your local running club and find out whether you can learn the techniques and tactics required to cut it as a sprinter or a middle distance runner. Or you might branch out into different sports altogether and use your running fitness to take part in a triathlon or adventure race. Just as you looked for advice when you took your first running steps, you'll need some background knowledge to safely develop your running career, which is where this book comes in.

Wherever your love of running and competition is taking you, the following chapters aim to help you on that journey. You'll find a brief history of the sport at elite level and how training methods have developed over the years, to inspire your love of running. There's practical advice on running faster in sprint and middle distance races, as well as the strength training you'll need to become powerful on the track. If you're staying with endurance running but would like to become really competitive, you'll find training advice for running at the 'sharp end' of the field and help with your nutritional and recovery needs. With training plans to get you started in ultramarathon running or triathlon, these pages contain everything you need to progress your running, increase your speeds and achieve your goals.

Right: Whether you run solo, in a group, or as part of a club, you will find it easy to fit training in to your daily life.

JOINING THE ELITE

Covering the basic areas of training can produce
good results in your running. However, to
produce great results, you will need to learn from the
greats. This chapter will tell you more about the history
of athletics, both professional and amateur, and
introduces some of the athletes and coaches who have
shaped the way that runners train today. You will also
learn about some of the special sessions that the top
runners use to give themselves an edge.

Above: Amateur runners can win races if they learn from top athletes' methods.
Left: You have to train fast to race fast – as these runners have learned.

A Brief History of Athletics

Today, it is difficult to imagine the world of running without the Olympic Games, the pinnacle of achievement for the athletes taking part. Yet the Olympics and the tradition of athletics that has grown up around them are relatively modern.

Organized athletics is thought to date back to about 4000BC, when short running races were held in Egypt. The Olympic Games as we know them today began much later.

Early days

The first records of the Olympic Games are from 776BC. The Games were held in honour of the Greek god Zeus, and were held at the site of an important shrine to him at Olympia. To begin with, the Games consisted of running events, including a short sprint of around 190m (620ft), the length of the stadium. Up to 40,000 spectators would watch. Women were not allowed to compete, but ran in games in honour of Zeus's wife, Hera, where they would race over a similar distance to the men.

Although officially the Games were held for amateur athletes – the only prizes received were garlands –

Below: The first Olympic Games were held in ancient Greece, attracting international athletes.

those who won were revered in their home communities. Then, as today, the event attracted competitors from many different countries, but unlike the modern Games, they did not stop during wartime. A temporary truce would be called when the Games took place every four years, so that athletes could compete against each other. However, over time, the Olympics fell into decline, until eventually the Games were banned in AD393 by the Roman emperor Theodosius.

Organized games were held elsewhere in the world, but the development of athletics was far from linear. The separate strands of amateur and professional athletics have caused contention from the sport's beginnings right through to the present day, and early athletics meetings in Britain were often more about prizes than participation. In the Middle Ages, running, jumping and throwing events were held to win food, money or clothing, although competitions also took place for fun. Britain's own Olympick Games began in 1612 in the Cotswolds, the idea of a local man named Robert Dover. These Games, which include throwing and jumping events as well as sack-racing, shin-kicking and a 5-mile cross-country run, still take place every year.

In the 18th century, the sport became more popular than ever, though focus had shifted to winning money. Walking and running events – pedestrian races – were common in Britain and America. Gentlemen would pit their footmen against each other, placing huge bets. Over time this grew into an industry, with professional pedestrians training and racing full time; races or exhibitions charged entry fees to spectators in addition to making money from gambling.

Above: The Olympic flame is taken around the world before the start of the modern Games.

The rise of the amateur athlete

By the 19th century, running had started to become a mass-participation sport. Tracks were built at sports grounds all around Britain, the first at Lords cricket ground in 1837. Sports became part of school life at public schools and universities both in the UK and in the USA, and friendly competition between colleges became popular. In contrast to the purely commercial pedestrian events, this movement toward amateur sports sprang from a belief similar to that held by the ancient Greeks many years before – that participating in exercise was both morally and physically beneficial.

In Britain, Oxford and Cambridge universities would compete against each other regularly, and American universities followed suit, with the Intercollegiate Association of Amateur

Time-keeping

It wasn't until the end of the 19th century that stopwatches were accurate enough to keep trustworthy records. Today it is difficult to imagine the sport of elite running without a focus on time, which is now sometimes deemed more important than the race result itself – an event might be considered a poor race if none of the competitors ran especially fast. But until the 18th century, runners simply raced against each other. Then, horse-racing clocks were used, and finally in 1855, a stopwatch with a second hand was invented, which meant that running races could then be timed to the second.

Athletes of America formed in 1875, and its first championships held the next year. Meanwhile, amateur athletics clubs were formed in London

Below: In 2004 the Olympics returned to their home in Athens, where the first modern Games were held in 1896.

Right: Baron Pierre de Coubertin founded the International Olympic Committee in 1894.

and New York, and gradually throughout the two countries. Governing bodies were set up: the Amateur Athletic Association (AAA) in England in 1880 and the Amateur Athletic Union in the USA eight years later.

Gradually the two countries began to compete against each other in friendly meetings, and against other European countries. This growing participation in amateur sports at English and American universities inspired a young French aristocrat, Baron Pierre de Coubertin, to come up with the idea of reviving the Olympic Games. General interest in the Games was increasing thanks to excavations at the original site in Greece, and de Coubertin was able to found the International Olympic Committee in 1894. He hoped that the first modern Olympic Games would improve international relations, and he placed the emphasis

not on winning, but on taking part; an ethos which holds true at the Games today. The first Games were held in Athens in 1896 – with the new event of the marathon, as well as traditional sprints, throwing, jumping and an arts programme – and were a huge success.

The Modern Olympics

The first modern Games in Greece in 1896 were a huge success. Athletics, and running in particular, has grown hugely in popularity since then, but as well as great advances, the Games have had their share of problems.

Following the success of the first modern Olympic Games in 1896, the Games of the second Olympiad in 1900 provided a shock for the IOC. Much to the annoyance of the Greeks, the Games were moved to Paris. This time they had to compete for the public's attention against the World Fair, being held in the city at the same time, and where the Greek public had greeted the Olympics with enthusiasm, Parisians were less forthcoming. The programme of events was spread over four months, and with so much happening in Paris it was not entirely clear what was part of the Olympics and what was not. As a consequence the full results were not compiled until several years later.

Athletics grows in popularity
The popularity of amateur athletics continued to grow, however, with more clubs opening around the UK, Europe and the USA. After the 1912 Olympics, it was

Below: Female athletes take part in the track and field events at the Olympics for the first time in 1928.

felt that athletics needed a governing body. To fulfil this need, the International Amateur Athletics Federation or IAAF (which now stands for International Association of Athletics Federations) was set up, with 17 member nations.

Meanwhile the Olympic movement grew, although World War I put a stop to the 1916 Games. In fact, despite

Above: Jesse Owens gives an American-style salute on the winners' podium at the 1936 Olympics in Berlin.

de Coubertin's original concept of promoting peace and understanding through sport, the Olympics became a reflection of political tensions around the world, with a difficult history of boycotts, spiralling budgets and late-running building works – areas which still pose challenges to the Games today.

However, the Games also held up a mirror to some of the more positive changes taking place worldwide. In 1928, following a campaign by the women's governing body, the Federation Sportive Feminine Internationale (FSFI), women were allowed to compete in track and field events at the Olympics for the first time. Progress was set back when, during the women's 800m final, many of the competitors collapsed from exhaustion, and the distance was deemed too demanding for women. From then until the Rome Games in 1960, women were not allowed to race farther than 200m; the women's marathon was not introduced until 1984.

Above: An official poster for the 1964 Tokyo Games, which were the first to be televised worldwide.

Dark clouds over the Olympics

The rise of the Nazi party in Germany, followed by World War II, had profound effects on the Games. At the 1936 Games, held in Munich and presided over by Adolf Hitler, the now-legendary black American athlete Jesse Owens defied Nazi beliefs with his incredible successes: gold medals in the 100m, 200m, long jump and 4 x 100m relay. The war put a stop to the Games until 1948, when the event was held again in London. The Games were a success in spite of ongoing food rationing, makeshift facilities and the banning of some of the countries that had been involved in the war, including Japan and Germany.

A worldwide event

Technological advances have had a huge impact on the Games. Records became more accurate in 1932 with the introduction of the photo finish and automatic timing for the 100m sprint.

In 1960, the Rome Olympics saw the Ethiopian Abebe Bikila win the men's marathon barefoot, marking the beginning of African athletes' dominance

Right: Ethiopian Abebe Bikila runs the marathon barefoot in Rome in 1980, going on to win the gold medal.

of distance running. These Games were the first to be shown on television, and the 1964 event was the first to be shown worldwide. This helped to drive interest in athletics even more, and to further commercialize the sport, so that the original amateur ideal was hard to maintain. At the same time, advances in athletic performances generally meant that athletes had to go to more extreme lengths to stay at the top, so many trained full-time and needed to earn money from their sport. However, it was not until the early 1980s that the IAAF relaxed the rules on amateurism.

The 1970s and 80s saw some of the most troubled years in the Games' history. The 1972 Munich Olympics were overshadowed by tragedy, when a terrorist attack on the Israeli team killed 11 athletes as well as 5 of the terrorists and 1 policeman. The event continued after a memorial service, with competitors agreeing that the attack should not stop the Games. The 1980 Games in Moscow were also indirectly marred by violence: in response to the Soviet Union's invasion of Afghanistan, several countries boycotted the event. The UK team ran against the wishes of their government, but this produced one of the greatest British competitions in Olympic history. The 1,500m specialist Steve Ovett beat Sebastian Coe in his favoured event, the 800m. Coe had his revenge by winning the 1,500m.

Above: American Joan Benoit celebrates winning a gold medal in the first ever Olympic marathon for women in 1984.

The biggest challenge faced by the sport now is a problem with banned substances, a controversy that has raged since the Canadian sprinter Ben Johnson was famously stripped of his 100m gold medal at the 1988 Games in Seoul. Having survived so much, however, there is no doubt that the competition, which attracts more than 10,000 athletes in 300 events, will continue to push the limits of human speed, strength and endurance.

Training Methods of Great Runners

To the experienced athlete today, it may seem that there is nothing new to learn in athletics training. Throughout the 20th century, experience, science and instinct honed the different approaches to running, and the foundation was laid for modern training.

The great coaches who developed and popularized new training methods were, in their time, often considered to be eccentric and, like all good leaders, their larger-than-life personalities often earned them as much criticism as praise. However, there is no question that runners owe a debt to these groundbreaking men (and many more besides).

Percy Cerutty (1895–1975)

Through the 1950s and 60s, Cerutty coached dozens of top Australian middle-distance runners. He led Herb Elliott to Olympic gold over 1,500m in 1960, and from 1956 to 1962, helped him become perhaps the best 1,500m and mile runner in the world. Although at the time Cerutty's methods were considered unusual at best, his training philosophy is one that would be recognized by many of today's runners.

Below: Olympic gold-winning athlete Herb Elliott climbs a rope under the strict supervision of trainer Percy Cerutty.

Above: Franz Stampfl (left) advises the Oxford University athletics team, 1954.

Cerutty took a holistic approach to training, and developed his own philosophy, which he called 'Stotanism' – a mix of 'Spartan' and 'stoicism'. He taught his athletes to accept both defeat and triumph, pain and success without showing their emotions. This would have required considerable strength of character, as Cerutty was a believer in intense, high-quality training to yield results. Instead of circuits or intervals around a running track, his athletes made use of the landscape around them, and Cerutty was famous for encouraging them to run up and down sand dunes to build strength (a method still used by runners from sprint to marathon distance). He also taught them to appreciate healthy eating, and was a keen practitioner of yoga.

Franz Stampfl (1913–95)

Although he took a very different approach to Cerutty, Franz Stampfl had just as much success: it was Stampfl who coached the British runner Roger Bannister to the first sub-4-minute mile in 1954. He left his native Austria for the UK in 1936 as an anti-fascist, and coached in Northern Ireland. On the outbreak of war, he was arrested and deported as an enemy alien. Stampfl was sent to Australia, but returned to the UK after the war. In 1955 he returned to Australia, where he coached a number of Olympic athletes including Ralph Doubell and Merv Lincoln.

Stampfl's scientific training methods came from his own experiences. He had been a skier in Austria, and on switching to track and field was shocked at how little training was done. He set about devising measured ways to teach the body to adapt to stress, most notably through intense interval sessions, during which careful notes were taken of time, distance, and the athlete's pulse. Stampfl's style was perhaps more dictatorial than Cerutty's, but the two shared a belief in the effectiveness of very hard training, and Stampfl would teach his athletes to train through pain.

Above: Peter Snell, coached by Arthur Lydiard, crosses the finish line first in the 800m at the 1960 Olympics.

Arthur Lydiard (1917–2004)

Although he struggled to find recognition for his methods during his career, Lydiard is often regarded as the father of modern coaching for middle- and long-distance runners. His programmes formed a blueprint for many of the training plans used by elite and recreational runners today.

Lydiard was a firm believer in 'base' training – that is, running long distances at relatively low speed to build a foundation of fitness. Even 800m or 1,500m runners, he argued, should run 100-mile weeks in the early stages of their training year. He also championed the idea of periodization, helping athletes to peak just before important competitions. However, his methods were considered extreme by some, and he clashed with the athletics establishment in his native New Zealand, and later in Mexico and Venezuela. Despite this there is no doubt that his ideas were successful: at the 1960 Olympics, his four New Zealand athletes (Peter Snell, Murray Halberg, Barry Magee and John Davies)

Right: Franz Stampfl coached Australian Ralph Doubell, winner of the 800m at the 1968 Olympics.

won six medals between them. While Lydiard's high-volume methods still attract criticism, his model of base training combined with hills and speedwork is still very much in evidence today.

John Smith (b. 1951)

In the past, it was believed that the best sprinters were born, not made, but the phenomenal speeds achieved by athletes in the last 25 years are as much a result of great coaches as great athletes. John Smith, a former international sprinter for the USA, has overseen numerous world and Olympic successes, including Maurice Greene's 1999 100m world record of 9.79 seconds. Working at the University of California and now through HSI (Hudson Smith International), Smith believes that great sprinting comes from relaxing, simplifying and breaking down the sprint. He breaks down the 100m sprint into five phases: reaction, drive phase (coming out of the blocks), transition (moving into full sprint), maximum velocity, and the finish or 'holding on' phase. Carefully moving through each phase, and spending as much time as possible in the maximum velocity phase, is crucial to the athlete's

Above: John Smith's coaching methods helped sprinter Maurice Greene to victory in the 100m in 1999.

success. As well as the physical aspects of sprinting, Smith teaches his athletes to stay humble when they win, and to stay confident when they lose. Smith's accessible methods and delivery continue to make him one of the best sprint coaches in the world.

Advanced Base Building: Twice-a-day Training

For endurance athletes at any level, building a base level of fitness is the first, crucial step to achieving full potential. For a runner, this means building up to running five or six days a week in the first instance.

If you want to make the jump from achieving average results to being a real contender in races, then you will need to increase your training volume. Some coaches place greater emphasis on base training than others, but all agree it is important. A coach might use the analogy of building a house: you have to build a strong, solid base before you can put the roof on, and the greater the height of the building, the wider and stronger the base must be. So, if you want to run fast over long distances (from the mile upward), you need a strong foundation of low-intensity training before you can add strength and speed elements.

Below: Train both in the morning and evening to spread out your running volume over the day.

The safest and most manageable way to increase training volume above the 75–105km (50–70 miles) per week mark – typical of recreational distance runners at a fairly high standard – is to switch to twice-a-day training. Increasing the volume in one session is both impractical in terms of fitting it into your working day, and dangerous in that it subjects your body to greater stress. Two runs a day allows your body time to recover in between.

The second run

Like all new elements of training, the second daily run must be added gradually to avoid injury and overtraining. First, it is important to be training once a day, every day. On your rest day, do a short recovery run

What base training does
• Trains your cardiovascular system and aerobic fitness
• Builds capillaries in the muscles, so more oxygen reaches them
• At low intensity, makes your body more efficient at using fat as fuel
• Improves oxygen use in slow-twitch and type IIa fast-twitch muscle fibres (which don't contract as fast as type IIb fast-twitch fibres, and can use the aerobic energy system as slow-twitch fibres do), so they will work better for longer

instead of resting completely. If you feel this is excessive or you are prone to impact-related injuries such as shin splints, you could swap to a longer

Twice-a-day training: tips

- Leave 4 or 5 hours between runs to give your body time to recover
- Do not add a second run either very early or very late in the day, as this will compromise your sleep, which in turn compromises recovery
- If you are prone to impact injuries, or start to suffer them while training twice a day, consider making your second session a cross-training session
- Remember you need to make up for the extra mileage by adding the necessary extra calories to your diet

Right: Elite marathon runners, such as Kenyan former world-record holder Paul Tergat, train two or three times a day.

training cycle, for example having one day off in ten instead of one in seven. Then add a second run to two of your training days, ideally days where your main session is speedwork.

The second run should be an easy run of 30 to 35 minutes. The easy run tends to work better as the first session of the day, when it can serve as a recovery run for the previous evening's session, and a 'wake-up' run before the main speed session. Running faster is naturally easier later in the day as this fits better with the body's biorhythms: the muscles are stretched out and warm and the metabolism is working more efficiently. Most runners also find it mentally easier to do the gentler run early on.

Adding more runs

Once you have become used to running in the morning of your speedwork days, add another two runs, then another two, until you are running twice a day, six days a week. On your long run day, stay at one run until you plateau, as running twice on this day results in a daily mileage that can be difficult for your body to recover from the next day. If you do introduce a second run on this day, consider limiting your long run to 30km (20 miles) at the very most. Complete the long run early and use the easy run later as a recovery session.

Above: On your long run days, try to stick to one run to allow your body to recover fully.

Who trains twice a day?

As you would expect, all elite distance runners train at very high volumes. For marathon runners, this means an easy week of not less than 160km (100 miles). The world's fastest marathon runners, including Britain's Paula Radcliffe and Kenya's Paul Tergat, will train two or three times a day even on easy days.

Twice-a-day training is not for everyone. Before you make the huge commitment, ask yourself what you hope to get out of it. If the answer is to complete a 4-hour marathon, it may not be worth it; If on the other hand this is your chance to break through from good club level to your national team, or to break a club record, then training this way for three or four years can help you achieve your dream.

Killer Speed Sessions

Successful runners have a high pain threshold. In order to progress, runners have to be prepared to push themselves to their limits. This may sound intimidating, but as long as hard training is planned carefully, it is one of the most exciting parts of being a runner.

The recreational runner will often find themselves going through year after year of the same kind of training, but elite athletes know the real value of sessions that test their psychological strength as much as their physical ability. These 'killer' speed sessions, which should leave you feeling as though you have nothing left in the tank, work for several reasons. They prove one of the most repeated rules of running: that in order to run faster, you have to run faster.

Below: Very fast speed sessions are psychologically difficult, so do them in a group or with friends.

This applies no matter what distance you are training for. Really hard training sessions help your body to develop the physiological backup to support you in fast races: your oxygen and fuel delivery systems will work much more efficiently, your running economy will improve, and you will become mentally tougher. These sessions also teach you about pace judgement, and races will feel easier as a result.

The training sessions that follow are split into three different groups: short, sharp sessions; middle-distance and threshold sessions; and long sessions. All these sessions are valuable, and you can adjust the

distances or times involved depending on exactly what you are training for. Various studies have been carried out on the true value and effects of speed training, and overall they don't offer any conclusions about which type of session most improves speed and fitness. However, speak to any group of runners and you will find that hard sessions in any form will, performed regularly and correctly, lead to gains in speed. You may also be surprised by how quickly results happen – just eight to ten weeks of fast work, providing you have the requisite base fitness, can result in personal best times over a number of distances.

Above: Keep a positive approach to speed sessions: don't see them as a chore.

Short, sharp sessions (reps up to 400m)

Half and half. Warm up with 10 to 15 minutes of easy running, then speed up to approximately your mile race pace for 30 seconds. Slow down to a 'cruising' pace – fast but relaxed, as opposed to easy – for 30 seconds. Repeat until you can no longer maintain your fast pace for 30 seconds, then cool down with 5 minutes of easy running or walking.

The 200 test. Even if you are used to speedwork, you are probably cautious about the number of reps you perform at one time. Elite athletes and their coaches rarely share that approach, however, and might run up to 40 short repetitions in one session. Emulate this with a 200m test: warm up with 10 minutes of easy running, then on a track, run the 200m straights at 800m pace and jog easily round the bends. Start with two sets of four laps (eight 200m repetitions), building up to three sets of eight laps with 5-minute recoveries in between. End with two easy laps.

Short pyramid. This is a shorter, faster version of the standard pyramid session. Start with a 10-minute warm-up and some stretches. Run 100m, 120m, 140m, 160m, 180m, and 200m starting at a 400m pace for the 100m stretch and running each rep slightly slower, finishing with your 1-mile pace for the 200m repetition. Run a 200m recovery between each repetition. Then, run a 5-minute recovery jog, and repeat the distances, this time running each as fast and evenly as you can. End with a 5-minute cool-down.

Below: Some speed sessions, such as the 'half and half', don't require a track.

Left: Use your 5K personal best as the basis for a tough 5 x 1,000m interval session.

Middle-distance and threshold sessions

Variety show. Mix the length of your intervals to recreate the bursts and lulls of races, and to get your body used to running hard when you are already tired. Warm up with a 10 to 15 minute jog. Then run 4 x 200m fast, 200m easy; 2 x 1,000m at mile race pace with 5 minutes recovery in between; then 1 x 200m, 400m, 200m, 800m, running the 200m and 400m at mile pace and the 800m repetition at 5K pace, and taking a 200m recovery between each. Cool down with a 5-minute jog.

5K 'personal best' session. Cheat your way to a new 5K personal best. Take your current 5K best time and round it down to the nearest minute, then divide this time by five (so if your personal best time is 19:21, round it down to 19, divide by 5 = 3:48). After warming up, run 5 x 1,000m at this split time with 400m easy recoveries in between. When this session becomes easy, take another 30 seconds off your new '5K personal best' (so 6 seconds off each 1,000m repetition), or reduce the recoveries to 300m.

Race pace session. Warm up, then run a 5–4–3–2–1 session at your race paces. Start with 5 minutes at 10K pace, then 4 minutes at 5K pace, 3 minutes at 3K pace, 2 minutes at mile pace, and 1 minute at 800m pace. Have a 90-second recovery jog between each repetition. When you have finished the set, do a 5-minute recovery jog then repeat, building up to three sets in total as you become fitter.

Below: At the track, mix up different lengths and speeds of intervals to recreate a race environment.

Pacing

These sessions assume that you are familiar with your race paces over a full range of different distances. You will need to use your recent race times to complete these sessions properly. Since very few runners race over all distances regularly, you can test yourself over the different distances by racing against three or four friends, or just running time trials on your own. If you are not familiar with a particular distance, try it three or four times over a few weeks (unless it is a marathon), as you will need to get used to pacing yourself at that distance before you can run your best time. It is also a good idea to have someone else time you, as this will provide you with a more accurate result.

Above: Completing some long runs at your marathon race pace is difficult but worthwhile.

Long-distance sessions

Marathon race pace. It is generally advised to complete your long runs at a very easy pace, but some runners – including many elite athletes – do theirs at or close to marathon race pace. You should aim to race a marathon just below your lactate threshold; if you have had this measured you can use a heart-rate monitor to stay five beats per minute below your threshold. Otherwise, aim to run at 80 per cent of your maximum heart rate. To start with, run the first 6.5–8km (4–5 miles) slowly, gradually increasing the amount of time you run at marathon race pace.

Dream marathon pace. Pick a marathon goal time that is significantly faster than your current time. In the middle of your long run, try three 1-mile runs at this 'dream' pace – so if you would love to run a sub-3-hour marathon, run three 6:56-minute miles – with half a mile of recovery in between. This teaches you to run hard in the middle of a long run, and shows you how it would feel to run at your dream pace.

Race sandwich. Running a short race is an ideal threshold session, so speed up your long run by running a race in the middle. Choose a local 5K or 10K race, and complete a 8–9.5km (5–6 mile) run just before – running as close to the start time as possible. After the race, stop just long enough to get through the finish procedure, then complete another 8–9.5km (5–6 mile) run.

Acceleration run. This session will be helpful if you find that you slow down at the end of long races, usually a result of allowing yourself to do the same thing in training. During any long run of 16km (10 miles) or more, promise yourself that you will run each of the last 8km (5 miles) 5–10 seconds faster than the previous 1.5km (1 mile) – so your last 8km (5 miles) might be run in 8:00 minutes, 7:55, 7:50, 7:45 then

Right: Look out for signs of overtraining and avoid killer training sessions if you are feeling too tired.

7:40 for the last 1.5km (1 mile). The idea is not to speed up drastically but to stay strong when you feel tired. It should also help you to pace the earlier miles in your run.

Skills and Drills

Many runners think of drills as being the sole preserve of the sprinter. In fact, skills and drills sessions are an essential cornerstone of sprint training as well as any sport that requires speed and agility, such as soccer or racket sports.

Drills are useful no matter what your distance for perfecting technique and giving you an edge. Research has shown, for example, that adding this kind of training improves 5K times and reduces your risk of injury.

Why practise skills and drills?

These sessions work by breaking down the running cycle into its constituent parts, slowing down the motion and improving the specific function of the muscles involved in efficient gait. The training works on your neuromuscular system, committing the movements to your memory so that when you speed up, the technique is carried through. It also trains your fast-twitch muscle fibres, which allow you to run at high speed. Your overall flexibility will be improved, which in turn lengthens your stride, and your reactions will become quicker so your leg turnover speeds up. Drilling can be as effective as conventional speedwork sessions, but without the risk of injury.

Below: Sports which require bouts of speed and direction changes, such as tennis, also use drills.

Above: Using drills gives you better running form, which should translate into faster race times.

Perhaps the best thing about incorporating these skills and drills sessions into your regular training is that these sessions are not too taxing, and so can easily be done on the same day as a harder session. You can use them as part of a warm-up for a track session or fast race – many of the moves act as dynamic stretching exercises, which will help prevent injury when you stride out fast – or you can do them a few hours after a long run, which should help to reduce any muscle soreness. Run through each drill four or five times in quick succession.

Though these exercises may look and feel strange at first, you'll be in good company if you start using them – many elite runners across all distances incorporate exercises like this into their training.

Hurdle walk

This slowed-down version of hurdling works on your hip flexibility, strength in your hip abductors and adductors (the muscles on the inside and outside of your thigh that help stabilize your pelvis and leg), and strength in your gluteals and hamstrings, which help to power you forward. Start slowly so that you get the technique right.

Hurdle skip

Once you are confident with the hurdle walk, speed up to a skip, bouncing on the balls of your feet as you go through the hurdles.

1 *Arrange six hurdles a stride apart in a straight line (use junior hurdles if you are worried about hurting yourself). Step over the hurdle confidently, keep your hips and torso square forward; push your lead foot out flat as if kicking a door open.*

2 *Plant the lead foot firmly on the ground as you bring your back leg over, trying to keep it as straight as possible. Beginners may find it difficult to stop the back leg trailing sideways so have someone else check your technique.*

This speeded up hurdle walk will improve your reaction times and use your fast-twitch muscle fibres. If you're exercising in a group (a good idea), go through in quick succession so that each person is forced to keep up the pace.

Side hurdling

1 *Keeping the hurdles in the same arrangement, a stride apart in a straight line, face them side-on and start by walking over sideways, one leg after the other.*

2 *After a couple of run-throughs, speed up to a skip, and when you reach the end of the hurdles, do not pause but skip the back leg straight back over and go back the other way.*

3 *Stay upright and tall throughout, use your arms and keep your legs almost straight. This exercise works on your hip flexibility and speed, as well as your rhythm and reaction times.*

Russian walk

You will need a flat, even stretch of ground about 20m (65ft) long for this drill. The motion is similar to the hurdle walk (without a hurdle, of course), but with greater emphasis on knee drive and arm action.

1 *Lead with your knee, pushing it high and in front of you, and keeping your foot flexed and taut; extend the lead leg, using the same kicking-open-a-door action as you used in the hurdle walk.*

2 *Plant your lead foot firmly on the ground without relaxing it. Keep your back straight and strong throughout and be careful not to twist your torso or hips. Keep your heels off the floor.*

Ankle walking

1 *This will improve your reaction to the ground, helping you to pick your feet up quickly. It also works on the strength and flexibility of your feet and ankles. Walk forward in small, quick, but smooth steps, staying on the balls of your feet.*

2 *Push your foot through a full range of motion as you move, from almost being on tiptoes to low down with your heel barely off the floor. Pump your arms back and forth in time to help you keep your balance and rhythm.*

Mini hurdles

The mini hurdles used for this drill are inexpensive, but you can use any small obstacles (20–30cm/8–12in high).

Arrange five mini hurdles in a line, 60cm (24in) apart. Run down the side of the hurdles, bringing the leg nearest them over each hurdle, planting your feet firmly on the floor. This will improve your foot speed and your arm and knee drive, so run through as quickly as you can.

Skills and drills – quick tips

- Do these sessions in a group if you can, as it will be more fun and much more challenging
- If possible, have a coach check your technique – it is easy to get it wrong and you will be teaching your body bad habits
- Inevitably, everyone trips over hurdles or ladders from time to time – treat it as a game and overcome your mental fear of the obstacles
- In all these exercises, arm drive is as important as the leg action, just as it is in running
- Make sure that you think about your entire body during drills, and don't let any part of yourself relax and drag through the movements
- Don't put too much emphasis on any particular drill, as this may result in an odd, unbalanced running style

Bungee drives

This exercise works on your knee drive and core strength. Do not set the resistance too high – this can cause injury.

For this exercise you need a bungee cord and a secure post or tree to attach it to. Attach the cord around one leg just above the ankle and walk forward until it is taut (but not pulling you backward). Drive the attached leg forward as you would in the Russian walk, pushing the knee high, keeping your hips facing forward and using your arms for balance and power. Do two sets of 10 on each leg, building up to three or four sets.

Speed ladders

Again, you can buy special rope ladders to place on the floor for this exercise, or you can simply draw out a chalk ladder or place rolled-up newspapers in a ladder formation.

1 *Place the speed ladder on the ground in an open space, where there is plenty of room. Staying on the fronts of your feet, start the exercise by running quickly through the speed ladder, placing one foot in the middle of each square and using your arms to drive the action.*

Below: Your local track should have a stock of hurdles and other equipment that you can borrow.

2 *Then run through the speed ladder, putting both feet in each square as you go. You can also run through sideways or even jump diagonally through the ladder's squares if you want to improve directional speed (for example, if you take part in any team sports).*

Skills and drills – equipment

At first it may seem as though there is a lot of equipment required for these skills and drills, however you will find that it is all relatively easy to obtain and often not too expensive.

SAQ International (SAQ stands for speed, agility and quickness) is one of the leading companies providing equipment for performing skills and drills. However, you can also perform most of these basic exercises without your own specialist equipment, by improvising. You could borrow hurdles from your local track or sports club and try using a fitness resistance band in place of a bungee. It is a good idea to set out all the equipment before you start, so you can easily do circuits of the drills, and you don't waste time between exercises.

Plyometrics or Jump Training

They may look like child's play, but the jumping and hopping movements of plyometric exercises are an essential part of many elite athletes' training plans. This type of training benefits athletes across a huge range of disciplines, from long-jumpers to football players.

Running is itself a plyometric exercise, so runners from sprint distance right up to marathon will see improvements with regular plyometric training.

Plyometrics (or jump training, as it is sometimes called) works by improving the explosive strength of the muscles, simulating running-specific actions such as accelerating or powering out of sprint blocks. These exercises recruit the fast-twitch muscle fibres used for pure speed. They also help to build overall strength, stride length, flexibility and proprioception (balance and co-ordination). The exercises don't take long and don't need to be carried out often – two short sessions a week is enough – yet they can have a huge impact on your race times. Although many amateur runners skip plyometrics, perhaps sceptical about its effectiveness, research has shown that groups who use this kind of training see greater improvements than those who don't.

One of the great things about plyometrics is that it is fun to do, but don't underestimate its effects – it is a very intense form of training, subjecting your muscles to forces many times greater than your own bodyweight. As such it is not a good idea to include plyometric training if you are new to running and exercise. The strain placed on your muscles, tendons and joints is likely to result in injury to unconditioned runners. When you do introduce plyometrics, treat it as you would intense speedwork or weight training; for example, don't do plyometric workouts on two consecutive days. A good time to do plyometrics is just before or after a speed session, ensuring you are fully warmed-up first, but if you become tired and find you can't perform the movements properly, stop and do the session another day. Poor technique will at worst result in injury, and at best have little training effect.

Quick tips for plyometric sessions

- Use a soft but even surface such as a track, lawn or mat in the gym
- Don't do plyometrics the day before a race, or two days in a row
- Engage your core muscles throughout the exercises
- Keep your landings light – land on the balls of your feet, allowing the natural rocking back on your heels to absorb force
- Perform the exercises with your absolute maximum effort, as they are designed to increase power
- Make sure that you allow at least 1 minute of rest between sets

Upper-body plyometrics

You can use plyometric exercises to build strength in your upper body, including your arms, chest and abdominal muscles. These exercises are used by athletes who require explosive power in their upper body, such as rowers and racket-sports players. Exercises might include plyometric push-ups, where you 'jump' up so both hands leave the ground at the top of the push-up, and throwing and catching weighted medicine balls. However, these exercises may be less effective than lower-body plyometrics, as the athlete does not use his or her full body weight during the exercise.

Below: Plyometric push-ups will build strength in your upper body.

Standing jump

1 *Stand with your feet shoulder-width apart, your knees soft and arms relaxed by your side. Jump straight up in the air, with just a slight bend of the knee so that your lower legs and ankles provide most of the force; swing your arms forward slightly as you jump.*

2 *When you land, go straight into the next jump as quickly as possible. Start with three sets of 5 and build up to three sets of 10.*

Squat jump

Long jump

1 Begin in a squat position, with your feet hip-width apart, back straight, knees bent and arms straight and behind you. Jump up into the air, straightening your legs and swinging your arms straight up above your head.

1 Start the exercise in a half-squat position (as for the squat jump, but slightly higher with less of a bend in the knees). Be careful if using a mat for this exercise, as the force of your landing may cause it to slip.

2 Swing both your arms behind you, then jump forward as far as you can. Bring your arms through so that they are out in front of you – the movement will help to carry you forward.

2 When you land, immediately lower back down into the squat position and repeat, without allowing your heels to stay down for more than a split second. Aim for two sets of five.

3 As you jump forward, keep your head up, looking straight in front of you rather than down at the ground. This will help you to jump a greater distance.

4 When you land, make sure you bend both knees to absorb the impact, then immediately crouch and bring your arms back for the next jump. Start with two sets of five jumps and build up to three.

Split jump

1 *Begin in a half-lunge position, with one leg in front and one leg behind you, your knees bent and hands either on your hips or by your sides. The front heel should be flat on the ground while the back heel should be raised slightly.*

2 *Lean back slightly from the hips and, pushing up from the knees, jump up into the air as high as you can. Switch your legs over while in the air, so that when you land again, your starting rear foot is in front of you. Repeat the jump, switching your legs over again.*

3 *As soon as you are back to the starting position, bend your knees and push up again for the next jump. Do two sets of four jumps on each side (so each set comprises eight jumps in total), building up to three sets.*

Jog with arm swing

Bunny hops

1 *Start the exercise on your right leg with the knee bent and your left leg bent up behind you, facing forward but with your arms out to the right (your left arm should be bent across your chest and your right arm should be straight out to the side).*

2 *Push up through your right leg to jump as high as possible, at the same time swinging your arms to the left and landing on your left leg. You can make the exercise harder by holding dumbbells. Repeat five times on each side and aim for at least three sets.*

Half-squat with your heels raised and hands on your hips. Jump up and forward, using your calves and ankles to push you. Land on the balls of your feet and keep ground contact to a minimum, hopping forward quickly. Start by hopping for 20m (60ft), then as you gain strength, rest, turn and hop back.

Depth jumps

1 For this exercise you will need a bench or step, approximately 30cm (1ft) off the ground. Begin the exercise by standing on the bench or step with your feet shoulder-width apart and arms hanging down by your sides.

2 Slowly step forward so that you drop onto the floor, bringing your arms back as you go, and as soon as the balls of your feet hit the floor, spring up in the air as high as you can, swinging your arms forward and up to help.

3 Do three sets of five. You can make the exercise more difficult by increasing the height of your step as you become used to the impact: a higher start will build strength in your legs, while a lower start emphasizes quick reactions.

Lateral lunge jumps

1 Start the exercise by standing next to a fairly low step – less than 30cm (1ft) high. Bring your right foot up onto the step with your left foot on the ground parallel to it, and with both your arms out behind you. Your right knee should be bent, while your left leg remains straight.

2 Pushing off with your right leg, jump up as high as you can into the air, so at the highest point of the jump, both legs are straight. Look straight ahead and throw your arms up in front of you as you jump. This movement will help you to jump higher.

3 Land with your left foot on the step, bringing your right foot down on the ground on the other side of the step, and then push up again as quickly as you can. Complete two sets of five jumps on each side (so each set has 10 jumps in total).

Improving Form and Cadence

Running is a completely natural activity. However, running efficiently and quickly does not come naturally to many of us, or even to elite athletes. While it is difficult to define a perfect running form, there are advantages to working on the way you run.

There are two basic elements to running faster: lengthening your stride, and increasing your running cadence (the number of steps you take in a minute). At the same time, you need to reduce wasteful movements such as side-to-side motion, or moving your head while running. There is some debate over whether it is possible, or even desirable, to radically alter your natural gait, and some of the world's fastest athletes have achieved huge

success with running styles that might be considered wrong. The way you run as an adult may have become ingrained as a child, or may have been affected by years of bad habits: carrying heavy bags on one shoulder, wearing poor quality shoes, running on a camber or compensating for old injuries. To become a more efficient runner, you must retrain your brain to forget these bad habits at the same time as learning a new way of moving.

Despite all the difficulties, if you want to squeeze every bit of speed out of your run, you can try breaking your running gait down to its simplest parts and teaching your body how to run better.

Improving stride length
To work on your stride length, you must first increase flexibility in the hip joint, hamstrings and gluteals, so that your thigh can move freely up to give a good knee drive for your leading leg. Regular and diligent stretching will help. Try exercises such as sprint bounding, strides, hurdle walking and the Russian walk. You will also need good core strength to hold your pelvis and back steady while you stride forward; without this the muscles around your hips will work harder to compensate for your weak core and this will eventually lead to injury.

Left: An efficient running style takes years to develop and involves your whole body, not just your arms and legs.

Form guide
• Always start by performing drills slowly to ensure that your technique is perfect, otherwise you will teach yourself bad habits
• Don't try to completely overhaul your running style if you are still seeing rapid improvements with your natural running style – you could do more harm than good
• Don't overemphasize work on one particular aspect of your gait, even if you feel it is a particular weakness. Remember that your whole body works together, and working on just one movement will throw out the balance of your movement

Improving cadence

It is very difficult to alter your natural cadence. However, there is a perfect cadence: most elite runners hit the ground about 180 times a minute (recreational runners tend to have a much lower cadence). You can measure your cadence using a speed and distance monitor, or if you don't have one, simply count the number of times one of your feet hits the ground in a minute and double this figure. Exercises to try to improve your cadence include downhill running, ladder drills and ankle walking. You can also try to improve your rhythm by making a conscious effort, although it is difficult to do this without shortening your stride. Use an electric metronome on a sports watch; try to reduce up and down movement while you run, and pump your arms more quickly (your legs will usually follow).

Exercises to improve overall form

As a runner you should already be doing at least three core-strength sessions per week. If you can find 15 minutes every day to perform a few core exercises, this will make a difference over time.

1 *Strengthen your gluteus medius muscles (small muscles that help stabilize your hips and move your legs apart) by lying on the floor with one leg on top of the other, your knees bent.*

2 *Very slowly raise the top leg, making sure that you keep your feet together, and then lower the leg down again. Repeat the exercise on both sides 10 to 15 times.*

Single-leg squats, performed slowly, will also improve your core stability and help reduce any side-to-side motion; do them while looking in a mirror to ensure your knee stays straight.

Improve your arm drive by practising swinging your arms back and forth while sitting up straight on a chair. This may feel a bit silly, but it really does work.

SPRINT AND MIDDLE-DISTANCE RACING

The advice given so far has largely centred on training for distance events of 5K and beyond, which is the most accessible type of running for most people. This chapter discusses some of the specialized training necessary to become a truly great sprinter and middle-distance runner, and the athletes that have inspired generations by pushing past accepted beliefs about how fast a human being can run.

Above: Usain Bolt wins the men's 100m in the 2008 Olympic Games, earning the title 'world's fastest man'.
Left: More than any other form of running, sprinting requires sharp focus and concentration.

Sprint Form and Drills

Good form is very important for all runners, but especially so for sprinters. At speeds of up to 48 kmh (30mph), where every hundredth of a second counts, every part of the body's movement must contribute toward moving forward.

A marathon runner might be forgiven for a tight shoulder or even a lopsided arm swing, but at the other end of the spectrum technique makes a much bigger difference. In sprinting there is no room for any wasteful side-to-side movements or energy spent tensing the neck, and biomechanical problems that seem minor in slow motion are exaggerated at speed. The key to great sprinting is relaxed speed.

The best sprinters make their motion look smooth and almost effortless, and the mistake many slower runners make is to 'try too hard' – running with

clenched fists, gritted teeth and hunched shoulders, which wastes energy and prevents a full range of motion. Watch a group of well-trained sprinters, and you will see that their style is often strikingly similar. This 'perfect' sprint form is developed over years of training using drills, visualization of correct technique and, crucially, the input of an experienced sprint coach.

Right: A sprinter in her starting blocks focuses on the track ahead of her, visualizing perfect form.

Sprint form

1 *The leading knee should drive high and forward, so the thigh ends up parallel with the ground. The toes of the lead foot should be pointed up, so that the foot is not allowed to 'drop' at any point during the cycle. Meanwhile, the back leg remains almost straight, not collapsing under the weight of the runner while on the ground, and extending right out behind the runner once off the ground.*

2 *The lead leg should land on the ball of the foot, in front of the runner but not so far forward as to produce an exaggerated stride, which leads to a braking effect. On striking the ground, the foot must pull the ground underneath the runner in a clawing action, without the heel dropping to the floor. As the other knee drives forward, the heel of that leg is brought up tucked under the runner before the lower leg is extended forward.*

3 *The support leg extends behind as before. Throughout the sprint, the torso should stay high and straight, the neck and face should be relaxed and the shoulders relaxed and down. The arms should both be bent at 90 degrees at the elbow, and should drive backward and forward, keeping in time with the runner's steps, helping to keep leg speed up.*

Starting from blocks

1 On your marks. *You need to experiment with the blocks to find the best position for you. Many sprinters find that a distance roughly equal to that from your ankle to your knee works well. You need to get the angle of the blocks right – the back block should be steeper. Start with your feet in the blocks, crouched, and your hands just touching the line, just wider than shoulder-width apart, with your thumb and fingers forming a bridge, and your arms straight but not locked.*

2 Set. *Keeping your hands where they are, with your thumb and fingers still in the bridge position, raise your hips up so that they are higher than your shoulders and you are leaning forward slightly – you should feel quite stable, but not exactly comfortable. Your front knee should be roughly at a right angle, while your back knee should make an angle of about 120 degrees. Push your feet hard into the blocks. Your face and neck should remain relaxed.*

3 Go! *Your reaction time here is crucial, but be very careful not to react before you hear the gun go off. Push hard out with your front leg, and drive the back leg forward at the same time, pushing up and forward, and leaning almost horizontally as you accelerate out of the blocks. Don't stride too far on your first step, or take steps that are too small; you need to move as quickly as you possibly can into your perfect sprint form.*

Sprint drills
Practice drills are as crucial for sprinters as they are for distance runners. Add these exercises to improve your sprint action.
Sprint bounds: over a distance of 50m (164ft), practise driving your lead knee forward and fully extending your back leg, using your arms to help the action as you would while running. Bound forward, slowly at first, speeding up as you perfect the technique. Over time, aim to cover the 50m (164ft) in fewer bounds.

Heel flicks: over a distance of 30–50m, (98–164ft) run forward on the balls of your feet, kicking your heel up to almost touch your bottom as quickly as possible. Ensure that your body stays upright and straight during the drill.

Harness runs: working in pairs, one runner holds the ends of a harness while the other walks forward in the harness until he feels resistance. Run forward against the harness, trying to keep as natural a gait as possible (instead of leaning right in to the harness).

Above: Include sprint bounds in your training sessions and you will soon see an improvement in your form.

Above: Keep your back straight and head up to get the best results from exercises like heel flicks.

Strength Training for Sprinters

You only have to look at a group of sprinters in the starting blocks to realize that strength training plays a huge part in their success. Compared with the lean, wiry build of a distance runner, sprinters look muscular and powerful.

While strength training plays an important role in all athletes' routines, for sprinters it is essential for developing the explosive power needed to drive them along at speeds of up to 10m (30ft) per second, and the control needed to ensure no energy is wasted along the way. Generally speaking, the shorter the specialist distance, the more strength is needed.

Top-level sprinters will push themselves through two or three weight-training sessions per week up to the competition phase of their year and, as with all training, they must be careful not to overload their muscles by strength training on the same days as their more intense running workouts. In race season, sessions are cut down and resistance is reduced.

There is some debate over how much emphasis should be placed on strength training. Some coaches feel that it plays too great a part in sprinters' training, to the detriment of out-and-out speed. Even at the elite level, sprinters should not spend more than an hour at a time on strength work, and should look on it as a complement to rather than replacement for specific running sessions. Too much strength work, particularly using weights, can increase bulk and body weight to a point where the athlete's power-to-weight ratio drops. Moreover, while resistance work increases the power of large muscle groups, research has shown that type IIb fast-twitch muscle fibres, which produce 'pure speed' (as opposed to type IIa which are not quite as fast), thrive when weight training is reduced. It is therefore important to include weight training and to reduce it just before the competitive season begins.

Press-ups

Works: chest, back, arms and core

Press-ups may be performed quickly or slowly, but always take care to ensure good technique is held throughout, with the abdominals contracted, and a full range of movement down to elbows bent to right angles and up to fully extended arms. To increase intensity, perform press-ups with your feet up on a bench.

Above: Whole-body strength plays a huge part in a sprinter's explosive power on the track.

Squats

Works: This exercise trains the muscles used to drive the legs forward during a sprint, including the gluteals, hamstrings and calves

1 *Increase the intensity by performing faster sets of half-squats (going down into a squat, but only coming halfway back up until the end of the set).*

2 *Single-leg squats work on core strength and balance. Keep your hands on your hips for balance, and lift one foot up off the ground before going into a squat.*

Step-ups

Works: gluteals, hamstrings, calves, quads

1 *Use a bench high enough that the lead thigh is parallel with the floor, with the knee bent at a right angle, just before stepping up. Put your hands on your hips or drive your arms up with your legs.*

2 *With your feet shoulder-width apart, step up with one leg and use that leg to push up on to the bench, bringing your other foot up next to the first, then step back down on the same leg.*

3 *Make the exercise more challenging and sprint-specific by driving the knee of the trailing leg high into the air before planting it on the bench. As you do so, rise on to the toes of your lead foot.*

Incline sit-up

Works: upper and lower abdominals, core and back

Using an abdominals board, perform sit-ups against gravity to increase their intensity, taking care not to pull your neck. Before you begin, ensure your spine is in a neutral position and engage your core muscles to avoid over-arching or flattening your back too much as you sit up. Try not to allow your feet to leave the floor or your quads to tense during the exercise.

Bridge

Works: gluteals, core

Lie on your back with your knees bent, feet flat on the floor. Push up through your heels, until your hips are in a diagonal line with your shoulders (which stay on the floor). Keep your abdominals tense, and hold the position for 10 seconds, then pulse up and down for 30 seconds, building up to 1 minute.

Weight Training for Sprinters

When training with weights, sprinters lift much heavier amounts than distance runners, but they should not attempt this kind of training without a general background in strength and conditioning.

Strength and fitness for sprinters might be achieved through special running workouts – for example, running on hills or sand; by using core strength exercises; or with regular bodyweight exercises. Plyometric sessions are also vital for sprinters. Strength training programmes need to be tailored to the individual sprinter, with particular attention to their specialist distance and training goals, but here are some of the basic exercises they might perform. It is important to have at least one spotter – a training partner to help you catch the weight if you become unsteady – during all weighted exercises. As you become stronger and the weights you use are heavier, this is especially important since there is a real risk of serious injury if you are unable to control the weight.

Weights and repetitions

It is important to have someone work out a weight-training programme for you: getting your weights wrong could lead to injury. The weights you lift and number of repetitions you perform will vary depending on where you are in your training year. Before you start it is useful to know your Repetition Maximum or 1RM: the heaviest weight you can lift once for a particular exercise. You need a spotter to help you work this out, an exercise professional who can make an estimate from your size and training history.

Once you know your 1RM, use it as a base measurement for deciding your workouts and for progressing to heavier weights.

Dumbbell arm swings

This will improve arm drive. With light dumbbells, watching your action in a mirror, stand up straight with your feet fixed and core engaged to hold your torso steady. Bend your elbows and pump your arms back and forth as quickly as possible, as if you were sprinting for 1 minute; rest 1 minute then repeat. Complete 4–6 sets.

Power clean

Watch points: Try to keep your abdominal muscles and back tight throughout this exercise to protect your back. Try not to push the weight out in front of you, instead jump it straight up.

1 *Start the exercise with your feet hip-width apart and the barbell on the floor just in front of you. Slowly bend down to grip the barbell with both hands – you should have your hands over the bar (with your knuckles pointing down) and about shoulder-width apart.*

2 *Lift the weight at a controlled speed by straightening your knees and back, keeping the bar close to your legs. Once the barbell has passed your knees, accelerate your motion. As the bar reaches mid-thigh level, jump the weight up, taking care not to push it out in front of you, but straight up.*

3 *Flip your elbows forward so you have an under-bar grip, and bring your body under the weight, allowing it to rest on your shoulders at the top of the movement. Drop into a half-squat to take the force of the weight, before immediately straightening up. Lower the barbell back to the ground slowly.*

Snatch

Watch points: Make sure you are steady before beginning the lift. Make the final flip movement of the weight as quick and smooth as possible.

1 The start is very similar to the power clean: feet hip-width apart, bend down to grip the barbell with your hands just wider than shoulder-width. Lift the barbell in a smooth motion as before, keeping it very close to your legs.

2 When you are standing straight, continue to lift the weight, keeping the same grip and allowing your elbows to move out to the sides.

3 As the weight reaches shoulder level, quickly flip it and drop underneath the bar, extending your arms and dropping right under the weight into a squat.

4 Slowly and steadily stand out of the squat to complete the lift.

Weighted step-up

Watch point: If the weight makes you lose control of the action, use a lighter one until you are able to step up straight.

1 The step-up exercise described earlier in this section can also be performed using a barbell. Lift the weight on to the back of your shoulders, using a towel to protect your neck if necessary.

2 Ensure you are steady and in control of the weight, with your feet hip-width apart and core tense. Step up on to a strong bench, slowly bringing your lead leg up onto the bench.

3 Slowly and steadily, bring your back leg up to stand square on the bench next to your lead leg.

4 Finally, lower the same leg down followed by the lead leg, so that you are back in the starting position.

Other weighted exercises

Since general strength and good overall conditioning is very important to all sprinters, you will also find it useful to include some of the standard weighted exercises used by other types of runners in your regular training sessions.

Alternatively you may decide to use heavier weights and fewer reps. Try to include different general exercises like weighted squats, lunges, calf raises and bench presses in your regular training routine.

Sprinting: 100m and 200m

The 100m sprint is the classic athletic competition, while the more specialist 200m involves a level of technical skill that only the best sprinters can master. The best sprinters start training young but anyone can learn to enjoy running as fast as they can.

For events that are over in less than half a minute, the short sprints take years to perfect. Here are the basics of 100m and 200m training.

100m

Running the 100m is not simply a case of running as fast as you can. Good sprinters break the distance down into a series of phases. First comes the start and acceleration phase (which is sometimes called the 'drive' phase). Practising reacting to the starting gun is crucial. Coming out of the blocks, the sprinter should drive hard, looking down at the track. From 30m to 60m, they will come up slowly and smoothly into the full sprint stride, fixing their eyes on the lane ahead. This 'tunnel vision' is essential to remain relaxed and in control – you should not be thinking about the people behind you. At 60m, sprinters reach their top speed, and the aim now is to hold on

Below: The sheer determination shows on the face of Jamaican Shelly-Ann Fraser (centre) as she goes on to win the women's Olympic 100m final, 2008.

Great athletes: Carl Lewis (b. 1961, Alabama, USA)

From a young age, Carl Lewis (Frederick Carlton Lewis) was determined to be a great athlete, and by any measure he succeeded. In 1999 he was voted Sportsman of the Century by the IOC. Throughout the 1980s and early 90s, he dominated both sprint and long jump at international level. He won five Olympic gold medals for sprinting (100m, 200m and 4 x 100m relays), and was three times the world champion at 100m, the first time in 1983 and last time in 1991. Lewis openly stated his intention to match Jesse Owens' 1936 record of four gold medals at one Olympic Games, and in 1984 in Los Angeles, he succeeded, winning the 100m, 200m, long jump, and leading the 4 x 100m winning relay team. His career was not without controversy, and when he accused Canadian athlete Ben Johnson of using drugs following defeat at the 1987 World Championships, many people thought he was bitter. However, he was

vindicated at the Seoul Olympics the next year, when Johnson, who had beaten Lewis to gold in the 100m, tested positive for steroids. Lewis was awarded gold. He retired in 1997.

Right: In 1999, Carl Lewis was voted Sportsman of the Century by the IOC.

100m and 200m: training examples

Date	Training phase	Theme	Weekly sessions
Oct–Dec	Conditioning	Strength and base building; less speed. Outdoor and off-road sessions	Aerobic training e.g. 3–4 mile easy runs Hill sessions (inc. sand dunes) 3 weights sessions per week: bodyweight and max weight sessions Core and flexibility work 2–3 skills and drills/plyometrics sessions
Jan–Mar	Speed endurance/ indoor season (e.g. racing 60m)	Learning to deal with lactate build-up, working in speed	2–3 endurance sessions (100–200m runs e.g. 5 x 100m, 4 x 150m; Pyramids: 110m, 120m, 130m, 140m and back down with long recoveries) 3 weights sessions: slightly lower weights than in conditioning phase Hills (1 session) 2–3 skills and drills/plyometrics; greater emphasis on power moves
Apr–May	Pre-season/ speed phase	Sessions move on to track; event specific practice	2–3 weights sessions: lower weights 2–3 skills and drills/plyometrics 3–4 speed and start practice sessions e.g. reaction sessions (coach starts with no warning, run 10–15m from blocks only); curve start practice; accelerations sessions e.g. 3 x 30m, each faster than last; 2–3 sets of 2–3 x 30–60m (long recoveries) 1–2 speed endurance sessions as above
Late May–Sep	Competition phase	Much lighter training volume, with races every week	Max 2 weights sessions per week with light weights 1–2 skills and drills sessions 2–3 speed and start sessions as above, but longer recoveries (12–15 minutes) e.g. 50m, 150m, 50m, 150m x 3; ladders 50m, 60m, 80m, 100m, 120m

to that speed as long as possible – usually from 60m to around 85m. From 85m to 100m deceleration is inevitable but during this 'finish' phase, the runner should relax and try to hold form. The finish is measured by the torso crossing the line, so a good lean forward is essential, but time it right: leaning too early slows you down.

Sure starts

Getting sprint starts right can help you to win races. When you are in the 'set' position you will react to the first sound that you hear.

This, however, can sometimes be a problem, as competition rules state that any reaction time faster than 0.10 seconds is a false start (because scientific research has shown that this is the fastest any human can truly react). In a race, one false start puts all the athletes on a 'yellow card', and the next athlete to commit a false start is disqualified, even if the first false start was not theirs.

200m

Most good 100m sprinters can also run a decent 200m, and vice versa, but the 200m is more technical. The first complication, which both 200m and 400m runners must deal with, is the curve start. It will take practice to find the right positions for your blocks (make sure no part of the blocks is in any other lane than your own). On the curve you cannot start at full speed, but you must learn to take it as fast as possible. Stay as far toward the inside of your lane as possible, bearing in mind that your speed will push you to the outside. As you come out of the bend, turn your right shoulder slightly to face the direction you want to run in (toward the finish), using the 'swing' effect of the curve to move up to full speed. Energy conservation is also crucial, as you have farther to run and need to limit your deceleration from 150m. Unlike in the 100m, a very small amount of lactic acid will build up, which is perhaps why 400m runners can excel at this distance.

Above: British 200m runner Linford Christie uses the curve in the track to accelerate up to full speed.

Sprinting: 400m

Running one lap of a track may not look difficult, but the longest of the sprint distances is uniquely tough. Pacing must be finely tuned as lactic acid builds up from 300m onward, resulting in heavy legs and inevitable slowing.

The special challenge of the 400m – not quite short enough to be a true sprint, not long enough to be a middle-distance run – is such that great 400m runners can come from a short sprint background (such as Michael Johnson – see box) or from a background of good 800m running.

At the elite level, the 400m is over in less than 50 seconds (less than 45 for male athletes), and there are a number of technical details to get right over that short space of time. Like 200m runners, athletes running the 400m need to practise curve starts, but they also have to negotiate a second bend at full speed (accelerating again at 200m), staying upright and not compromising form.

Endurance is another important aspect of good 400m running, and something that doesn't really come into the shorter sprints. Physical speed endurance is clearly crucial, and 400m runners need a strong aerobic base as well as plenty of lactate-threshold-level training to learn to deal with the discomfort of running with lactate build-up. Mental endurance is just as important, since athletes will have to 'dig in' over the last 100m to win the race; they need to be able to shut off from the other lanes and run their own race.

Above: Toward the end of the 400m, athletes need to stay strong and mentally focused on their own race.

Date	Training phase	Theme	**400m: training examples** **Weekly sessions**
Oct–Dec	Conditioning	Building aerobic base and strength	20–45-minute off-road runs 2–3 sessions weights (moderate, not as heavy as for 100m/200m training) 1–2 sessions skills and drills/plyometrics Hill and stair running session Long, slow intervals e.g. 4 x 600m, short recoveries (2–3 minutes)
Jan–Mar	Speed endurance	Learning to cope with race pace over long periods	Hill/stair running session 2 weights sessions 2–3 plyometrics/skills and drills sessions Speed sessions of 5–10 reps of 100–600m e.g. 8 x 150m, 2 x 600m; 4 x 450m close to race pace; negative split runs 200m, rest 200m x 3–4 (total distance should be not be more than 3–4 times race distance)
Apr–May	Speed/pre-season	Moving almost all training on to track	2 weights sessions, reduced intensity 2 skills and drills/plyometrics (shorter sessions) Curve-start practice sessions Pure speed sessions as for 100m/200m e.g. 50m fast, 50m relaxed fast x 6 with long recoveries Event sessions: completed at race pace, but with race distance broken down e.g. 2 sets of 3 x 350m with 50m fast, 150m relaxed, 150 as fast as possible
Jun–Sep	Competition	Regular racing, reduced training volume	1–2 weights sessions, light weights 1–2 skills and drills sessions Event sessions e.g. 200m, rest, 200m at race pace 320m as race practice; add 10–12 seconds for predicted time (used by Clyde Hart, Michael Johnson's coach)

Great athletes: Michael Johnson (b. 1967, Texas, USA)

From 1991, when he won his first World Championship title over 200m, until his last international competition at the Sydney Olympics in 2000, where he won gold at 400m and as part of the 4 x 400m relay team, Michael Johnson won a total of five Olympic golds and nine World Championship golds. His 200m world record of 19.32 seconds, set at the Atlanta Olympic Games in 1996 was the biggest improvement ever over the previous record, which he had also set earlier that year. His record was only broken in 2008 by Jamaican Usain Bolt. Johnson achieved what many thought was impossible, winning gold at the 200m and 400m in the same Olympics. His 400m world record, still standing in 2008, was set in more remarkable circumstances. Coming into the 1999 World Championships in Seville, Johnson had suffered injury problems, which meant he had barely raced that season, and only qualified by virtue of being the defending champion. He won in 43.18 seconds, and went on to lead home the American 4 x 400m team to gold. Throughout his career, Johnson's strange running style puzzled onlookers: his stiff, straight back and short strides going against ideal sprint form, but with seven of the ten fastest-ever 400m times to his name, few would argue that it worked against him.

Right: Michael Johnson was extremely talented, winning gold in 200m and 400m at the same Olympic Games.

Pace the race

Different athletes develop different strategies for pacing the 400m. As with longer races (right up to the marathon) they are faced with a choice between running out fast and 'holding on' – which is always a risky plan – or starting the race relatively slowly and gradually speeding up. When considering the second approach, it is worth bearing in mind that it will be impossible to run a negative split (the second 200m faster) in a good field, and it can be mentally very demoralizing to watch the field run away from you at the start. Ideally, athletes should train to run with as even a pace as possible. This is incredibly difficult and requires acute awareness of your own limits and your pace. The last 100m of the race is inevitably always the slowest, as your body simply cannot cope with the level of oxygen debt, but great 400m runners will learn how to minimize this slowing down – a perfect example being Michael Johnson's world-record run in 1999: he ran the first 200m in 21.22 seconds, and the second in just 21.96 seconds.

Below: Jeremy Wariner (centre) of the USA, on his way to winning the men's 400m at the IAAF World Championships in Athletics, 2007.

Hurdles

For schoolchildren trying clear them for the first time, hurdles is probably the most fearsome athletic event. Even in later life we use hurdles as a metaphor for barriers and difficulties in our lives. A good hurdler will almost literally take the hurdle in his stride.

Hurdle races should be seen as sprints with added low obstacles rather than a series of 'jumps'. In fact, much of the power, speed and strength required of a hurdler crosses over with straight sprinting, and many athletes will be proficient at both (hurdlers often start out as promising sprinters). The main differences are that a hurdler needs excellent rhythm, and advanced flexibility. Losing your rhythm in a hurdling race can cost valuable hundredths of a second. As well as building basic speed and power (using similar training to sprinters), hurdlers must learn to fix their stride rate: over 110m (or 100m for women), they'll take 8 strides from the start to the first hurdle, then 3 strides between hurdles; over 400m, 20 strides should reach the first hurdle and they'll aim for 13–14 strides between barriers. Throughout the race, the aim is to keep as close to sprint form as possible so that the forward action remains fast and smooth.

Right: The short distances between the hurdles mean that getting into a good rhythm is essential for athletes.

Great athletes: Ed Moses (b. 1955, Ohio, USA)

The career of American 400m hurdler Ed Moses started abruptly, but his incredible run of good form lasted for almost ten years. Having trained as a straight sprinter, Moses had only raced the 400m hurdles once up until March 1976, but using fewer strides between hurdles than his rivals (12–13), he was able to take his personal best over the 400m event from 50.1 seconds at the start of 1976, to 48.30 going into the Montreal Olympics that summer. He went on to win the gold medal at the

Games, at the same time setting a new world record of 47.64 seconds. The following year Moses began an incredible winning streak that lasted up until 1987, winning 122 races consecutively including another Olympic gold and two World Championships titles. Moses ended his career with an Olympic bronze medal in Seoul in 1988.

Right: American hurdler Ed Moses won 122 consecutive races in just under 10 years.

Hurdle sequence

1 *At the start, the lead leg should be in the back block. The start is identical to a sprint start, driving hard out of the blocks with the body almost horizontal. However, hurdlers must come up into full sprint stance (running upright and 'tall') sooner, within four or five strides, in order to take the first hurdle well.*

2 *On take-off, the athlete drives the lead leg up and forward knee-first (as in sprinting and hurdle drills), extending but not fully straightening it. The knee should not lock, as this makes it difficult to land smoothly and keep running. At the same time she drives her opposite arm forward for balance.*

3 *Coming over the hurdle, the hurdler leans her torso forward at the hips, keeping her centre of gravity as low as possible. Remember the aim is to clear the hurdle efficiently rather than 'jump' over it. The trail leg should be tucked up and pulled through as tightly as possible, ready to drive forward for the next step after landing.*

4 *There is no pause on landing, as the lead foot touches down and 'claws' the ground (as in sprinting). The hurdler pulls upright again as she lands, to continue sprinting. As in straightforward sprinting, twisting and side-to-side movements are wasteful and disrupt running rhythm, so the aim is to keep the hips and shoulders square on to the hurdles throughout.*

Relays

The sprint relays offer more than an extra chance for a podium finish. Sprinters' success usually depends on their ability to block out other athletes, so the relays are a completely different kind of running, based on team training and team success. Athletes who can perform smooth, fast handovers can sometimes beat those whose actual sprint speed is faster.

The 4 x 100m relay is perhaps the trickiest as the baton changes must take place without looking (turning back to look at the team-mate before you leads to too much slowing). It is crucial that athletes get to know each other's speed and style. The handover takes place inside a 20m box, and the runners are allowed to begin running up to 10m before that box (in the 4 x 400m, they cannot start outside the 20m change zone). In training, they will work out where they need to start from and where their team-mate will hand over. To avoid running too far with the arm out waiting for the baton, the preceding athlete should call out when they're ready to hand over. At handover, the baton should be held at the very end so there is plenty for the next runner to take hold of. Handing the baton down into the upturned palm of the next runner allows for the fastest change, but is not as secure as handing 'up' in to a down-turned hand. In the 4 x 400m, the receiving athlete turns to look at their preceding team-mate to receive the baton, but has a harder task judging when to start running, and accelerating away from their inevitably slowing predecessor.

Below: The baton handover is slower in the 400m relay.

Speed Endurance for Middle-distance Running

In races up to 400m, the athlete's focus must always be on speed and on 'true' speed endurance. Middle-distance track races may look pedestrian in comparison, but running a sub-2-minute 800m or a sub-4:30 mile are as much about the 'endurance' as the speed.

The first time a runner races as fast as he can around two or four laps of a track, and experiences the shattering fatigue of the last few hundred metres, it becomes clear just how important tough training is to run these distances well.

To understand this unique challenge, it is important to be aware of the different energy systems that give runners the power to propel themselves forward at different speeds. Broadly speaking there are two energy pathways: the aerobic system, which uses oxygen to produce energy from the fuel in your muscles, and the anaerobic system, which does not use oxygen. (The anaerobic system can be broken down further into the alactic or immediate anaerobic system – which

Right: Tatyana Tomashova of Russia wins the women's 1,500m race at the World Athletics Championships, 2005.

Great athletes: Maria Mutola (b. 1972, Maputo, Mozambique)

Above: Maria Mutola was a reluctant runner at first, but went on to win nine world titles at 800m.

A somewhat reluctant athlete at first, Maria de Lurdes Mutola has become one of the most successful female 800m runners ever, with 11 world titles to her name (including 7 indoors) and 2 Commonwealth golds. Mutola had been a keen footballer at school and, even when persuaded to try track running, initially found the training too intense. However, her talent for middle-distance events quickly became obvious and, at just 15 years old, she competed in her first Olympic Games (in 1988) – though she was knocked out in the first heat of the women's 800m. Mutola gained funding from the IOC and moved to the USA to train, and it was after this that she began her domination of the event. She finished fourth at the World Championships in 1991, and went on to win five Championships medals from 1993 to 2003 (including three golds). She won Olympic gold at the Sydney Games in 2000, but was beaten to the title in 2004 by her training partner Kelly Holmes. Over the next two years, Mutola suffered injury problems, but in 2006 she again won gold at the World Indoor Championships, and she competed at the World Championships in Osaka in 2007, finishing third in her semi-final. Mutola's only world-record performance was over 1,000m in 1995, but while she may not be the fastest 800m runner ever, her consistency and longevity as an athlete are matched by few.

provides intense bursts of energy for up to 4 to 6 seconds – and the lactic or short-term anaerobic system, providing energy for up to about 90 seconds of intense exercise.) While sprinting predominantly uses the anaerobic pathway, middle-distance runners make much greater use of the aerobic systems so need more aerobic training. The real difficulty, though, is getting the balance right – more than for any other running events, speed and endurance are of equal importance.

Building a base of aerobic training is essential for 800m and 1,500m runners, and during the winter months their training may not be dramatically

Below: Rashid Ramzi, 800m winner at the 10th IAAF World Championships in Athletics, knows that this race is as much about endurance as it is about speed.

Use of energy systems over different distances		
Race distance	Aerobic	Anaerobic
100m	8%	92%
200m	14%	86%
400m	30%	70%
800m	57%	43%
1,500m	76%	24%
Marathon	99%	1%

different to that of long-distance runners. Long, slow runs and relatively slow intervals with short recoveries help to condition the body ready for the serious speedwork that takes place in the lead-up to competition.

Anaerobic training could take up two or three sessions per week, though the total distance covered at this level would not amount to many miles (doing too much anaerobic training

leads to fatigue and an increased risk of illness and injury). Middle-distance runners race at or close to their maximum heart rate, and well beyond the lactate threshold, so they must train their body to adapt to these stresses. Use a mixture of very fast, fairly short reps – 200m to 400m – with long recoveries, and longer intervals at race pace or slightly slower, with shorter recoveries. The British athlete Sebastian Coe and his coach and father Peter believed that not quite allowing the heart rate to recover between intervals, so allowing lactic acid build-up, was a good way to help the body adapt. Speed endurance sessions from both sprint programmes (400m) and from 5K programmes are useful, as the middle-distance runner needs the pure power of the sprinter combined with the endurance and lactate tolerance of the longer-distance athlete.

Middle-distance Racing: 800m and 1,500m/Mile

The mile was long regarded as the 'classic' distance in athletics, a baseline measure of an athlete's speed and skill. These days, thanks to the metric system, it is rarely raced – certainly at international level – and the 1,500m has taken its place.

Sitting in between the 'metric mile' and the sprint events are the tough two laps of the 800m. Athletes who are able to compete well in one middle-distance are usually able to compete well in both distances, though they may choose to specialize in one or the other.

Both the 800m and the 1,500m require impeccable pace judgement, so participating athletes must know precisely how fast they can run each lap – the aim being to run as evenly as possible, with a 'kick'

over the last lap. However, in a race situation, of course, you may not always be able to run the race exactly as you would choose to do. Runners with a stronger endurance base might choose to push the pace early on, while those with a sprint finish might prefer to head straight to the front of the pack and try to keep the pace down.

Right: Some long-distance, easy running to develop aerobic fitness is vital for middle-distance running.

	Middle-distance racing: 800m & 1,500m schedule			
	Session one	**Session two**	**Session three**	**Session four**
Week one	4 x 400m Race Pace (RP); 6–8 mins rest; repeat	8 x 200m faster than race pace, with 200m easy between; then 2 x 600m RP with 2 mins recovery	5K/3-mile time trial or race	60 mins easy
Week two	6 x 300m just faster than RP, 3 mins recoveries	150m, 200m, 250m, 300m, faster each time, then back down, with 200m recoveries	5K time trial	60–80 mins easy
Week three	5 x 400m RP with 2 mins recoveries; 6–8 mins rest; repeat	2 x 1,000m just slower than RP, with 3–4 mins recovery	1,500m/1-mile time trial	60 mins easy
Week four	5 x 400m RP with 1 min recoveries; 6–8 mins rest; repeat	800m, 1,000m, 800m at mile pace with 2–3 mins recoveries	15–20 mins at lactate threshold pace	60–80 mins easy
Week five	4 x 400m at RP, 50 sec recoveries; 5 mins rest; repeat	150m fast, 50m easy x 6; then 2 x 800m at RP with 2 mins recovery	1,500m or 800m time trial	60 mins easy
Week six	8 x 300m at RP with 1:30–2 mins recoveries	2 x 1,000m at mile pace with 3–4 mins recovery	5K time trial	60 mins easy
Week seven	4 x 400m at RP with 1 min recoveries; 6-8 mins rest; repeat	200m fast, 200m easy x 6; then 2 x 800m at mile pace with 400m recovery	1,500m/1 mile time trial	60 mins easy
Week eight	As week 7	2 x 1,200m at mile pace, 5–6 mins recovery	15 mins lactate threshold, then 4 x 200m RP with 400m recoveries	1,500m or 800m race

Great athletes: Sebastian Coe (b. 1956, London, UK)

For British athletics fans, Sebastian Coe is an icon of a golden era of running, along with his 'rivals', Steve Ovett and Steve Cram. Though an 800m specialist, Coe's two Olympic gold medals were at 1,500m and he remains the only man to successfully defend this title at consecutive Games.

Coe won his first major competition at the 1977 European Indoor Championships, taking gold in the 800m. His first (much-hyped) race against Ovett, the European Championships 800m in 1978, was an anti-climax. Ovett won silver, Coe bronze. The next year, Coe set world records at 800m, 1,500m and the mile. In total he set 11 world records during his career.

The Moscow Olympics in 1980 saw Coe and Ovett winning each other's events – Ovett won the 800m, leaving Coe with silver; then Coe won the 1,500m, with Ovett in third place. In 1984, despite having been ill most of the previous season, Coe defended his 1,500m title, beating Steve Cram. Cram, four years his junior, eclipsed Coe the following year, beating his mile world record. In 1986 Coe was ranked number one in the 800m for the fourth time but he was not picked for the 1988 British Olympic team.

On leaving athletics, Coe went into politics but nevertheless remained heavily involved in sports. Most recently he led London's successful bid to host the 2012 Olympic Games.

Above: Sebastian Coe holds up the Union Jack after winning the Olympic men's 1,500m final, 1984.

The best way to prepare for this is to include regular time trials or low-key races in your training. Training in a group can, of course, help you to work on your speed and tactics, but only running against a group of real competitors can teach you how to run your own race.

Below: The 1,500m can be a very tactical race as competitors must decide where to position themselves in the pack.

And don't just race the distance you've chosen to specialize in: 800m runners should try the odd 400m sprint and 1,500m or even 3,000m race, while 1,500m runners should have good 800m speed and endurance up to 5,000m.

Middle-distance race schedule

Runners should have a solid base of aerobic training, hill running, weight training, plyometrics and

perhaps also some cross-country racing, built up over the winter months. Note that only the four key sessions are given in the schedule, on the other days athletes should use easy aerobic running, plus some weights or plyometrics sessions if desired.

Below: Wilfred Bungei (centre-right) of Kenya wins in the men's 800m final at the 2008 Beijing Olympics.

Middle-distance Racing: 3,000m and 5,000m

The 5,000m and the less common 3,000m are a natural step up from the classic middle-distance races. For young athletes, learning real endurance on the track in these races provides a solid background for moving on to the 10,000m and on to long-distance events.

The training for 3,000m and 5,000m track races is very similar to training for a 5K race on the road (the obvious difference being that almost all sessions take place on a track). However, the difference between a 5,000m and a 5K race is marked and each setting requires a completely separate mental approach. In a road-based 5K, the front runners might not see anyone else after the first few kilometres, but on the track the athletes are never far away from each other, and this makes the whole race much more intense. Moreover, unlike a

Right: In a 5,000m event, concentration and planning are important to ensure that you don't get boxed in by other athletes.

	Monday	Tuesday	Wednesday	Thursday	Friday	Saturday	Sunday
			5K: advanced schedule				
Week one	3 easy	2 x 1,000m with 3 mins recoveries	5 easy with 4 x 100m strides at end	4 x 800m with 2 mins recoveries; 8 x 200m with 200m recoveries	Rest	6km (4 miles) inc. hills	10–13 km (6–8 miles)
Week two	4 easy	3 x 1,000m with 3 mins recoveries	5 easy with 150m hard, 50m easy x 4 at end	6 x 400m with 90 secs recoveries; 1,200m x 1	Rest	8km (5 miles) inc. hills	13–15km (8–9 miles)
Week three	4 easy	1,000m; 1,600m; 1,000m with 3 mins recoveries	4 easy with 6 x 100m strides throughout	6 x 800m with 90 secs–2 mins recoveries	Rest	6km (4 miles) inc. hills	13–16km (8–10 miles)
Week four	4 easy/ cross-train	1,200m, 1,600m, 800m with 3 mins recoveries	5 easy with 150m hard, 50m easy x 6	200m, 400m, 800m x 2 with same distance recovery	Rest	6 km (4 miles) inc. 10–15 minutes easy fartlek	13–15km (8–9 miles)
Week five	4 easy/ cross-train	1,200m x 3 with 2 mins recoveries	5 easy with 4 x 100m strides at end	6 x 400m with 90 secs recovery; 4 x 200m with same recovery	Rest	8km (5 miles) with 6 x 100m strides at end	10–13km (6–8 miles)
Week six	3 easy	3 x 1,000m with 2 mins recoveries	Rest/cross-train	6km (4 miles) with 150m hard/50m easy x 4 at end	Rest	3 easy/rests	5K race

Above: Tariku Bekele and Abreham Cherkos of Ethiopia lead the field at this stage in the 5,000m 2008 Olympic final.

road race, there are no distractions on the track: with lap after lap of running, athletes are forced to concentrate on the task in hand. A 5,000m or 3,000m runner needs to think about where he sits in the pack for most of the race; run to the front too soon, and you risk 'blowing up' in the last few laps, but stay too far back and you risk being boxed in by other athletes, unable to break away from the pack.

Track races can become quite aggressive, and runners can expect to be elbowed, tripped over and spiked as the

competition heats up. The pace is usually faster than on the road, because of the flat, smooth surface of the track, the close proximity of the other competitors, and the relatively sheltered environment. Because of this, even for the longer track distances, runners should work on leg speed, training at mile or 800m pace two or three times per week.

5,000m and 3,000m: advanced schedule

To train for these distances, follow the Advanced 5K Schedule, but do all of your speedwork on the track and aim to race once or twice a week. Even low-key races with relatively small fields will give you the competition practice you need to become accomplished at the distances.

Include some of the following sessions to build leg speed and confidence on the track:
• 6–8 x 400m at mile speed with 90-second recoveries
• 6–8 x 300m at 800m speed with 2-minute recoveries, reducing recovery if these become too easy
Longer speed ladders at 3K pace:
• 1,000m; 1,200m; 1,400m; 1,600m and down again with 2-minute recoveries
• 150m hard, 50m easy, to exhaustion.

Year-round practice

The track season is fairly short, running from May to September. In the winter, cross-country racing helps runners from middle-distance upward to keep their summer speed. Without track markings, and with the added challenge of harsh, muddy terrain and poor weather, athletes toughen up and learn to race each other rather than the clock. Find out more about cross-country running in Cross-Country and Trail Running.

Great athletes: Wang Junxia (b. 1973, Jiaohe, China)

Wang Junxia's brief career as an international runner came to an end at the age of just 23, but some of her best performances on the track remain unbeaten. Having won the 10,000m at the world junior championships in 1992, her best year was 1993, when she became the world champion at 10,000m in Stuttgart. She went on to break the world record at the distance by 42 seconds, running 29:31.78. A month later, she set a world record at 3,000m (8:06.11).

However, Wang's career was not without controversy: her then-coach, Ma Junren, was criticized for his harsh treatment of his athletes, which included forcing them to run a marathon a day at altitude; he was later (in 2000) expelled from the Chinese Olympic team after six of his athletes tested positive for illegal substances. Some have claimed that Wang's world records, in particular her 10,000m time, could not have been possible without drugs, though Wang maintains this is not the case.

In 1994, she left Ma behind, and at the 1996 Olympics she won gold in the 5,000m in 14:59.88 and silver in the 10,000m in 31:02.58. However, years of intense training had taken their toll, and Wang retired the following year on a doctor's advice.

Below: Wang Junxia's track career was brief but brilliant, with a 10,000m record of 29:31.78.

ADVANCED LONG-DISTANCE RUNNING

When you have been running for several years, the idea of covering 5K or even 32km (20 miles) in one go does not seem daunting. However, there is a huge difference between completing long distances comfortably, and actually racing them. This chapter looks at how to race long distances successfully, covering everything from perfecting your pre-training nutrition, to training your mind to deal with the loneliness that comes with long-distance running.

Above: Once you know you can conquer a distance comfortably, you'll be racing against the clock.
Left: At the front of the pack, long-distance races are fast and tactical.

Perfect Nutrition Planning

The diets of elite athletes are almost as legendary as their 240km (150-mile) training weeks. As an amateur you don't need to start eating egg-white omelettes for breakfast, but if you want to maximize your potential, then nutrition planning is as important as the training itself.

If you decide to completely devote yourself to your sport, then unfortunately you will need to accept a few difficult facts. Heavy training sessions mean that you will burn more calories than the average person, but this does not mean that you can eat whatever you want. In fact, it is more important than ever to cut out unhealthy junk food and ensure that every mouthful you eat has some nutritional benefit for your body. It is also worth noting that the best athletes are slightly underweight – research has suggested that sprinters and hurdlers are 5 to 6 per cent lighter than the average 'ideal' weight, while long distance runners should be about 15 per cent lighter. However, runners need to balance the need to stay lean with a tendency to become obsessive (which can lead to eating disorders) and the need to eat enough to fuel their training.

Below are some guidelines for planning what you eat. If you are committed to taking a detailed approach to your diet, you will need to keep a precise food diary and plan what you are going to eat each day (research has shown that people who keep long-term food diaries are more

Above: Even though sprinters like Linford Christie look bulky, they are 5 to 6 per cent lighter than the average ideal weight.

Right: Marathon runner Paula Radcliffe has a very low BMI of 18, thanks to careful nutritional planning.

Featherweight champions

There do seem to be different ideal body types for different kinds of sport, and for different forms of running – on the whole, the longer the distance, the smaller and lighter the athlete should be, but what is really important is the athlete's power-to-weight ratio. It is no good being extremely light if this means that you have no muscle. The great athletes listed below would all be considered light by average standards.

Athlete	Distance	Height	Weight	BMI
Herb Elliott	Mid distance	1.79m/5'10.5"	66.6kg	20.8
Seb Coe	Mid distance	1.78m/5'10"	54.4kg	17.2
Linford Christie	Sprint	1.89m/6'2.5"	77kg	21.6
Paula Radcliffe	Long distance	1.73m/5'8"	54kg	18.0

Above: You can work out how many calories you need to maintain or lose weight easily.

successful at losing weight and maintaining their ideal weight). Weigh and measure your portions, and check the packaging of any pre-packed foods to note what they contain. When working out how much to eat, remember to account for all the exercise you do or don't do – you may need to alter your intake if you become injured and miss sessions.

How much should you eat?

Whether you want to maintain your current weight or lose weight, you need to know approximately how many calories you burn every day. First, work out your resting metabolic rate (RMR).

For men aged 18 to 30:
(weight in kg x 15.3) + 679
For men aged 31 to 60:
(weight in kg x 11.6) + 879
For women aged 18 to 30:
(weight in kg x 14.7) + 496
For women aged 31 to 60:
(weight in kg x 8.7) + 829

Right: The men's finalists in the 2008 Olympic marathon knew the value of strict dietary planning.

Remember, your RMR is the lowest number of calories your body needs simply to function. Any activity you do during the day must also be accounted for, so if you have a sedentary job (for example you work at a desk or behind a store counter), multiply your RMR by 1.4; if you do some activity, such as walking around, multiply it by 1.7; or if you are very active (outside of your sports training), multiply it by 2. Then, add to this figure the approximate number of calories you burn during your training. You can measure this using a heart-rate monitor (you will need to input details such as your weight, age and maximum heart rate); if you work out in the gym, you can use the read-outs on the machines' consoles as a rough guide.

If you want to lose weight, reduce the number of calories you consume by 10 to 20 per cent, aiming to lose around 0.5kg (just over a pound) each week. Lose weight any faster and you risk slowing down your metabolism and losing muscle mass. You should aim to cut calories from fat – one gram of fat contains nine calories, so it is energy-dense food. Restrict your carbohydrate intake to

Above: Middle-distance runner Herb Elliott weighed just 66.6kg at the peak of his athletics career.

about 60 per cent of your calories, reduce your fat intake to around 20 per cent of your daily calories, and at the same time aim to slightly increase your protein intake to 1.6g per kg of body weight.

High Protein Diets

Running and controlling your body weight go hand in hand – running is a great way to lose weight, and losing weight is a good way to improve your running. It is no surprise that many runners will diet at some point, and high protein diets are an obvious choice.

Athletes know that they need more protein than the average person to build muscle; they may also have heard that high-protein diets are a fast and effective way to lose unwanted fat. However, to avoid having a detrimental effect on your running, you must be careful about what kind of high-protein diet you follow.

High protein vs low carbohydrate

The recent popularity of high-protein, low-carbohydrate diets such as the Atkins model stems from the idea that dieters can eat as much as they want (in terms of calories) and still lose weight fast. The theory behind these diets is that cutting down carbohydrates reduces insulin resistance, which in turn stops the body from storing energy as fat. High-protein, low-carbohydrate diets force the body into a state of ketosis, in which fat is broken down and

Below: American sprinter Carl Lewis followed a vegan diet, showing you don't need meat for protein.

chemicals called ketones are released into the bloodstream. In the initial stages of the diet, carbohydrate intake drops to around 20g (¾oz) of carbohydrate a day (remember that athletes usually get 60 per cent of their calories from carbohydrates – at least 250g/9oz a day). After the first two weeks, small amounts of carbohydrates are gradually reintroduced.

These diets are highly controversial. Some scientists say they work only by creating a calorie deficiency, largely because the choice of foods is so restricted. Others go as far as to say they are dangerous, leading to kidney and heart problems. What is certain is that these diets are not suitable for athletes. Studies have shown that people on low-carbohydrate diets have far lower endurance levels than those on diets with a high or standard level of carbohydrate. Dehydration is also a risk on low-carbohydrate diets, a clear disadvantage for runners. So, runners wishing to lose weight and gain muscle should think in terms of high protein rather than low carbohydrates.

Above: As a serious runner, you should view food as fuel, and consider the nutritional benefit of every meal.

The benefits of protein

It has been suggested that a sports person requires more protein than the average person regardless of their weight goals. An averagely active person needs around 0.8g protein per kg of body weight, but that rises to 1.2 to 1.4g/kg for middle- and long-distance runners. If you are trying to lose fat, that figure rises again to around 1.6g/kg. It is useful for several reasons. For long-distance runners, protein can be a useful extra fuel when your carbohydrate stores (as glycogen) run down. It helps build muscle, making you a more powerful, stronger athlete, and to repair damaged muscle, not only when you are injured but after any tough or long run. Protein is useful for athletes trying to lose weight, as foods that are high in protein are more difficult to digest, thus

Left: Be careful not to cut down on your carbohydrate intake, since it gives you energy for fast running.

raising your metabolism slightly. It also makes you feel full for longer: some scientists believe this is due to a hormone, PYY (peptide YY), being released into the blood by cells lining the gut when you eat protein, which tells your brain you are full. Protein also helps prevent you from losing muscle when dieting (a common side effect).

Eating enough protein

Keep a detailed food diary for a week, and work out how much protein you currently eat. The chances are you will be far short of your required amount as an athlete. It can be difficult to work out how much protein you are eating at every meal, so if you don't have time to plan every gram, try adding protein: sprinkle nuts and seeds on your breakfast cereal, or have a low-fat yogurt with your usual snack of fruit. If you need to cut calories from elsewhere, try to cut down on fatty foods rather than protein or carbohydrates.

Contrary to popular belief, vegetarians do not suffer from lack of protein or poor quality protein (the great sprinter Carl Lewis was a vegan), but you may need to plan your meals more carefully. In fact, whether you are vegetarian or not, you should aim to get your protein from a range of sources. Different foods contain different types of protein, so a combination is best.

Below: Sprinkle sunflower, pumpkin or sesame seeds on to cereals or salads to instantly increase your protein intake.

Below: A 100g (3¾oz) serving of oily fish provides one-quarter to one-third of your daily protein requirement.

Protein-rich food:	
Food	**g protein/100g**
Lightly roasted turkey meat	33.6
Lean grilled (broiled) beef	29.5
Grilled (broiled) mackerel	29.5
Sunflower seeds	18.8
Walnuts	14
Quorn	12
Kidney beans	8.3
Tofu	8
Medium egg (per egg)	8
Low-fat yogurt	5.5
Baked beans	5

Perfect Light Meals

Most professional sportspeople have nutritionists to carefully plan their diets, from breakfast first thing in the morning through to the smallest snacks during the day. The rest of us have limited expertise to draw on, but these simple meals should help keep you on top form.

In an ideal world you would spend hours every day training, and the hours in between planning the rest of your life around your training, including a meticulous diet. The reality for most amateur athletes is that life – and work – gets in the way, and food is often the first aspect of our lifestyles to suffer. Your light meals are often more rushed than your main meal of the day, so it's easy to grab a pre-packed salad or bagel without checking what's in it. Unfortunately these convenient meals aren't designed with runners in mind, so you'll often find them full of hidden fats and refined carbohydrates, and lacking in the essential nutrients you need to run well and stay healthy.

But it doesn't take much time or effort to make your own healthy light meals; soups can be prepared in large batches and frozen in portions so you won't need to spend time on them on busy working days. These recipes are all low in fat but high in protein and slow-release energy; serve them with wholegrain bread for the extra carbohydrates and calories you'll need for training. Each of the following recipes makes four modest portions (for which the values are given) or three more generous servings.

Lean Scotch broth

200g/7oz pearl barley
1 onion
2 carrots
*1 small swede (rutabaga), peeled
and chopped*
1 leek, washed and chopped
115g/4oz/1 cup cabbage, shredded
*75g/3oz/½ cup boiled lean gammon
(smoked or cured ham), cubed*
salt and pepper

Put the pearl barley in a pan with 1.5 litres/2½ pints/6¼ cups of water. Bring to the boil, cover and simmer for 45 minutes. Add all the remaining ingredients and simmer for 30 minutes.

Nutritional information per portion: Energy 280kcal/1176kJ; Protein 11.3g; Carbohydrate 50.4g; Fat 5.3g.

Hearty bean soup

15ml/1 tbsp olive oil
1 onion, finally chopped
1 clove garlic, peeled and crushed
2 large carrots, peeled and chopped
*2 x 400g/14oz cans mixed beans,
drained and rinsed*
400g/14oz can chopped tomatoes
15ml/1 tbsp tomato purée (paste)
5ml/1 tsp dried oregano
5ml/1 tsp dried basil
1 bay leaf
150ml/¼ pint/⅔ cup red wine

Heat the olive oil in a large pan, and then fry the chopped onion and garlic together in the oil until soft. Add the chopped carrots and continue to cook gently for 4 or 5 minutes, until the carrots start to soften. Next, pour in the mixed beans and the chopped tomatoes, stirring, then add the tomato purée, dried oregano, dried basil, bay leaf and red wine, and stir well.

Gently simmer the soup for 10 to 15 minutes, then remove the bay leaf. At this stage, you can either transfer the soup to a food processor and process until smooth, or if you prefer a chunky texture, serve as it is.

Nutritional information per portion Energy 238kcal/1000kJ; Protein 17g; Carbohydrate 52g; Fat 4.1g.

Eating on the run

In an ideal world, everyone would eat a homemade lunch every day, but life gets in the way, often forcing us to grab a pre-packed lunch. If you have to do this, make sensible choices:
• Good sandwich fillings are lean proteins such as chicken or fish, or eggs or falafel for vegetarians. These will keep you full and help to keep your muscles healthy.

• Try to avoid buying over-complicated sandwiches or those which contain an obvious dressing – this will probably contain mayonnaise and will increase the fat content
• Go for wholemeal (whole-wheat) or seeded bread rather than white for slow-release energy
• If you choose a soup or pasta dishes with sauce, go for tomato-based or cream-free varieties.

Tofu and wild rice salad

175g/6oz/1 cup basmati rice
50g/2oz/generous ¼ cup wild rice
250g/9oz firm tofu, drained and cubed
25g/1oz preserved lemon, finely chopped
30ml/2 tbsp fresh parsley, chopped

For the dressing:
1 garlic clove, crushed
10ml/2 tsp clear honey
10ml/2 tsp of the preserved lemon juice
15ml/1 tbsp cider vinegar
15ml/1 tbsp olive oil
1 small fresh red chilli, finely chopped
ground black pepper

Cook the basmati rice and wild rice in
two separate pans. Whisk together
the dressing ingredients in a bowl.
Add the tofu, stir to coat and marinate
for 20 minutes. Fold the tofu, marinade,
preserved lemon and parsley into the rice,
check the seasoning and serve.

Nutritional information per portion:
Energy 284Kcal/1185kJ; Protein 9.6g;
Carbohydrate 47.6g; Fat 5.8g.

Homemade falafel

2 x 400g/14oz cans chickpeas in water,
   drained and rinsed
1 small onion, chopped
2 garlic cloves, peeled and crushed
30ml/2 tbsp fresh coriander (cilantro),
   finely chopped
30ml/2 tbsp flat leaf parsley, finely
   chopped
5ml/1 tsp ground cumin
5ml/1 tsp garam masala
salt and pepper
10ml/2 tsp vegetable oil
sesame seeds, for sprinkling

Place all the ingredients except for the
salt and pepper and vegetable oil in
a blender and blend to a dough-like
consistency (you may need to add a dash
of oil to help the mixture stick together).
Season, making sure that you mix the
seasoning in well. Take the falafel 'dough'
out and roll it into golf-ball sized rounds,
then pat down so they are flat. Sprinkle
with sesame seeds.

   Heat the oil in a pan over a medium
heat and fry for 2 minutes on each side,
until they are crispy. Serve with a leafy
salad, tomato salsa and low-fat plain
yogurt as a dip. You can keep the falafel
for up to two days in the refrigerator
before the frying stage, fry them as
required and use them in sandwiches.

Nutritional information per portion:
Energy 183kcal/768kJ; Protein 9.7g;
Carbohydrate 22.9g; Fat 6.5g.

*Left: Wholegrain bread is a great source
of the extra carbohydrates your body
will need while in training.*

Tomato and lentil dhal

30ml/2 tbsp vegetable oil
1 large onion, finely chopped
3 garlic cloves, chopped
1 carrot, diced
10ml/2 tsp cumin seeds
10ml/2 tsp mustard seeds
2.5cm/1in fresh root ginger, grated
10ml/2 tsp ground turmeric
5ml/1 tsp mild chilli powder
5ml/1 tsp garam masala
225g/8oz/1 cup split red lentils
800ml/1½ pints/3¼ cups vegetable stock
5 tomatoes, peeled, seeded and chopped
juice of 2 limes
60ml/4 tbsp chopped fresh coriander
   (cilantro)
ground black pepper
25g/1oz/¼ cup flaked (sliced) almonds,
   toasted, to serve

Heat the oil and cook the onion for
5 minutes. Add the garlic, carrot, cumin
and mustard seeds, and ginger. Cook for
5 minutes. Stir in the ground turmeric,
chilli powder and garam masala, and cook
on a low heat for one minute, stirring.
Add the lentils, stock and chopped
tomatoes, and season with ground black
pepper. Bring to the boil, then reduce the
heat and simmer, covered, for 45 minutes,
stirring occasionally.

   Stir in the lime juice and 45ml/3 tbsp
of the coriander. Cook for a further
15 minutes until the lentils are tender.
Sprinkle with the remaining coriander
and the flaked almonds.

Nutritional information per portion:
Energy 326Kcal/1372kJ; Protein 16.9g;
Carbohydrate 43.8g; Fat 10.5g.

Perfect Main Meals

Complicated cooking is probably the last thing you feel like doing after a hard day at work or looking after your family, but let low energy stop you from eating well and you'll get caught in a vicious circle. You need to eat well to refuel no matter how long your day has been.

There is no need to spend hours and hours slaving away in the kitchen to cook the perfect main meal that will help you recover from both your chores and your training. And you certainly don't need to cook separate meals for yourself and your family; in fact children are likely to benefit from a well-balanced runner's diet, although of course you will need to make smaller portions of food for younger children.

These healthy versions of classic family main meals are low in fat, but high in protein and slow-release energy to help you recover from a hard day's work and training.

The portions in these recipes are all quite modest, but if you have worked out your nutritional requirements you can adjust the recipes to provide you with more energy if necessary.

Below: When you are training hard it is important to find the time to sit down and eat a healthy, balanced meal.

Pasta with fresh tomatoes and basil

500g/1¼lb dried penne
5 very ripe plum tomatoes
1 small bunch fresh basil
60ml/4 tbsp extra virgin olive oil
salt and ground black pepper

Cook the dried pasta in a large pan of lightly salted boiling water for 12–14 minutes, or according to packet instructions, until tender.

Meanwhile, roughly chop the tomatoes and tear up the basil leaves. When it is cooked, drain the pasta thoroughly and return it to the clean pan. Add the tomatoes, basil and olive oil, and toss to mix together thoroughly. Season with salt and freshly ground black pepper and serve immediately.

COOK'S TIP
If you cannot find ripe tomatoes, roast those you have to bring out their flavour. Put the tomatoes in a roasting pan, drizzle with oil and roast at 190°C/375°F/Gas 5 for 20 minutes, then mash roughly.

Nutritional information per portion:
Energy 552kcal/2336kJ; Protein 16.3g;
Carbohydrate 96.9g; Fat 13.8g.

Low-fat chilli con carne

15ml/1 tbsp vegetable oil
1 onion, finely chopped
1 garlic clove, peeled and crushed
300g/11oz lean beef steak, cubed
100g/3¾oz/scant 2 cups mushrooms
1 red (bell) pepper, chopped
400g/14oz can tomatoes
400g/14oz can red kidney beans
15ml/1 tbsp tomato purée (paste)
5ml/1 tsp paprika
5ml/1 tsp ground cumin
5ml/1 tsp chilli powder
500g/1¼lb sweet potatoes
200g/7oz/scant 1 cup low-fat natural
*   (plain) yogurt*

Heat the oil in a large pan. Fry the onion and garlic in the oil until soft. Add the beef, mushrooms and pepper and continue to cook until the meat is browned. Add the canned tomatoes, kidney beans, tomato puree and spices. Simmer for 20 minutes. Meanwhile, cut the sweet potatoes into wedges and bake in the oven at 200°C/400°F/Gas 6 for 20 minutes. Serve the chilli with the wedges, topped with the yogurt.

Nutritional information per portion:
Energy 380kcal/1596kJ; Protein 31.1g;
Carbohydrate 45.6g; Fat 9.4g.

Stir-fried prawns with noodles

130g/4¹/₂oz rice noodles
30ml/2 tbsp groundnut (peanut) oil
1 large garlic clove, crushed
150g/5oz large prawns (shrimp), peeled
15g/¹/₂oz dried shrimp
15ml/1 tbsp Thai fish sauce
30ml/2 tbsp soy sauce
30ml/2 tbsp palm sugar (jaggery) or
    light muscovado (brown) sugar
30ml/2 tbsp fresh lime juice
90g/3¹/₂oz/¹/₂ cup beansprouts
40g/1¹/₂oz/¹/₃ cup peanuts, chopped
15ml/1 tbsp sesame oil
chopped coriander (cilantro), 5ml/1 tsp
    dried chilli flakes and 2 shallots,
    finely chopped, to garnish

Soak the noodles in a bowl of boiling water for 5 minutes, or according to the packet instructions. Heat the groundnut oil in a wok. Add the garlic, and stir-fry over a medium heat for 2 minutes, until golden brown.

Add the prawns and dried shrimp to the pan and stir-fry for a further 2 minutes. Stir in the fish sauce, soy sauce, sugar and lime juice. Drain the noodles, then add to the wok with the beansprouts, peanuts and sesame oil. Toss to mix, then stir-fry for 2 minutes. Serve immediately, garnished with the coriander, chilli flakes and shallots.

Nutritional information per portion:
Energy 312Kcal/1299kJ; Protein 11.8g;
Carbohydrate 35.8g; Fat 13.3g.

Chicken fried rice

30ml/2 tbsp groundnut (peanut) oil
1 small onion, finely chopped
2 garlic cloves, chopped
2.5cm/1in piece fresh root ginger,
    peeled and grated
225g/8oz skinless chicken breast fillets,
    cut into 1cm/¹/₂in dice
450g/1lb/4 cups cold cooked white long
    grain rice
1 red (bell) pepper, seeded and sliced
115g/4oz/1 cup drained canned corn
5ml/1 tsp chilli oil
5ml/1 tsp hot curry powder
2 eggs, beaten
spring onion (scallion) slices,
    to garnish

Heat the oil in a wok, and stir-fry the onion for 1 minute, then add the garlic and ginger and cook for 2 minutes more. Push the onion mixture to the sides, add the chicken to the centre of the wok and stir-fry for 2 minutes more.

Add the rice and stir-fry for about 3 minutes, until the chicken is cooked through. Stir in the red pepper, corn, chilli oil and curry powder. Toss over the heat for 1 minute. Stir in the beaten eggs and cook for about 1 minute more. Serve in bowls and garnish with the spring onion slices.

Nutritional Information per portion:
Energy 356kcal/1500kJ; Protein 21g;
Carbohydrate 46.4g; Fat 10.9g.

Low-fat meat-free moussaka

15ml/1 tbsp olive oil
1 garlic clove, peeled and crushed
1 onion, finely chopped
1 red (bell) pepper, chopped
250g/9oz/generous 1 cup red lentils
100ml/3¹/₂fl oz/scant ¹/₂ cup red wine
400g/14oz can tomatoes
10ml/2 tsp dried oregano
2 large aubergines (eggplants)
40g/1¹/₂oz unsalted (sweet) butter
600ml/1 pint/2¹/₂ cups skimmed milk
150g/5oz/1¹/₄ cups plain (all-purpose) flour
200g/7oz half-fat Cheddar cheese, grated

Fry the onion and garlic in half the oil until soft. Add the pepper and cook for 1 minute. Add the lentils, red wine tomatoes, and oregano and bring to the boil, then reduce the heat and simmer for 20 minutes. Slice the aubergines and brush with the remaining oil, then grill (broil) for a few minutes until soft.

Melt the butter, then add the flour and fry for a few minutes over a low heat. Gradually add the milk, stirring. Slowly bring to the boil to thicken the sauce, then add most of the cheese, keeping a handful back. Layer the lentil mix and the aubergine in a baking dish, ending with an aubergine layer. Pour the cheese sauce over the top and sprinkle with the remaining cheese. Bake for 30 minutes at 220°C/425°F/ Gas 7 until brown on top.

Nutritional information per portion:
Energy 527kcal/2213kJ; Protein 31.1g;
Carbohydrate 57g; Fat 18.9g.

Sports-specific Fuel

Ideally, the fuel needed to run well and recover quickly would come from natural sources. However, consuming enough energy and nutrients from normal food is not practical, particularly for longer races: special energy drinks, bars and gels are designed for this.

To overcome the problems of eating on the run, manufacturers have come up with a huge range of drinks, energy gels and bars to help athletes take on food and fluids as easily as possible. Many runners struggle with these products at first, as they often taste sweet and artificial, which can be difficult to tolerate when two hours of running has left you feeling nauseous. However, it is well worth practising taking on energy foods as you run, because they will help you perform better and protect you from illness and injury afterward.

Your muscles' preferred choice of fuel is glycogen, a quickly-accessible form of carbohydrate. However, you can only store enough glycogen for between two and two and a half hours of running. For an amateur marathon runner that will only take them 29–32km (18–20 miles). At this point, as the body switches to fat for fuel, many runners

Below: Take advantage of drink stations along the race route to ensure that you don't become dehydrated.

Above: Energy bars will provide plenty of calories but are best eaten before a race rather than during.

'hit the wall' – they temporarily run out of energy as the body works to convert fat into usable energy. The aim of sports fuels is to feed your body carbohydrate so that it doesn't need to switch to fat burning (you can also help yourself by training your body to use fat as fuel – for example using long, slow runs – so that your glycogen stores are preserved for longer).

When running a long-distance race, you should aim to consume about 40 to 60g of carbohydrate per hour. It can be difficult to stomach carbohydrates on the run, so you should never try eating them for the first time during a race. Practise taking on carbohydrates in training, using whatever brand you plan to use during the race. Sports products fall into three categories:

Energy bars

These are the most energy-dense form of sports foods, but as such they are more difficult to digest. They are best used before a race, or during long, slow races, such as ultramarathons or stage races. (However, studies have shown that eating an energy bar and taking on water with it is as effective in delivering energy as sports drinks or gels.) Typically they provide carbohydrates from rice, oats and maltodextrin. Beware of bars with high levels of glucose, which can cause a spike in your blood sugar, and fructose, which can have a laxative effect. Many bars also contain some protein (for recovery, and slow-release energy), and may also include nuts, chocolate or toffee to make them taste better. From a functional point of view, the simpler the better – more than 5g of fat, 5g of fibre and 10g of protein will make the bar difficult to digest. They usually provide 30 to 60g of carbohydrates per bar, which is enough for an hour of exercise.

Below: You can buy powdered sports drinks and add water – some races will allow you to leave these at water stations.

Above: All races must provide water, and many bigger events will also have sports drinks on offer.

Energy gels

A good compromise, energy gels are a more compact way of carrying your fuel and are easier to digest than bars. The downside is that they can be messy to take, and you usually need to drink some water with them (to make the mixture isotonic and easily absorbed). However, they only provide around 15 to 30g of carbohydrates per portion, so you will need at least two for each hour of exercise. On a marathon that could add up to six to ten gels, which is a lot to carry and a lot to stomach. Gels usually contain fast-release carbohydrates from sugars, so it is important to take them at regular intervals (every 20 to 30 minutes) to keep your blood sugar levels steady.

Sports drinks

Faster athletes usually choose drinks over gels and bars because they are much easier to take on at high speeds. At many big races, sports drinks are available around the course so you don't have to carry anything – check which brand will be used and practise drinking it in training. Otherwise, see if you can make up your own drinks and

Left: Practise using your chosen food and drink during training to make sure you react well to it.

have them placed at water stations around the course. Most sports drinks, mixed up correctly, provide an ideal 6 to 8g of carbohydrate per 100ml – you will need to drink between 750ml and 1 litre per hour.

Preventing illness

Many athletes complain that they are more likely to catch colds and bugs in the days just after a big race. This is because the harder you train and race, the more your immune system is suppressed. Part of the reason for this is that the stress hormones which are released when your body switches to fat burning for energy block the action of some types of white blood cells, which form part of your body's defences against illness. By keeping your body's carbohydrate levels topped up, you will reduce the need for fat to be used as fuel, and also help prevent stress hormones from being released, so fuelling your run will not only help you run well on the day, but will aid your recovery afterward.

DIY Training Fuel

Runners tend to have a better awareness of what they put into their bodies than other people, so it is strange that many of them come to rely on manufactured training fuels, which can be full of highly refined sugars, especially when these recipes are so easy.

Even energy bars and drinks that contain only natural ingredients – and there are plenty of examples of these on the market – can taste artificial. For this reason many athletes prefer not to use them at all, sticking to water. In doing so they are missing out on the hugely important benefits of staying well-fuelled during tough training sessions and long races. However, if you are prepared to invest a little time, you can easily make your own energy snacks and drinks at home.

All of these recipes deliver more than 30g of carbohydrates, roughly the same as a store-bought energy gel, but because of their slightly higher fat content (in most cases), they will take a little longer for your body to digest. As such they are better for eating before you begin a training session rather than while you are out running, with the exception of the natural isotonic drink, which will provide you with an almost instant energy hit.

Above: Mixing your own natural energy drink from fruit juice and water at home is cheap and easy.

Fruit flapjacks
The oats in this bar should help to calm pre-race nerves; the sultanas and honey give a moderate-GI energy release, while the ground ginger (which is optional) should help to stave off nervous nausea.

200g/7oz/scant 1 cup butter or margarine
225g/8oz soft light brown sugar
30ml/2 tbsp clear honey
300g/11oz/2½ cups jumbo oats
150g/5oz/1 cup sultanas (golden raisins)
2.5ml/½ tsp ground ginger

Melt the butter, sugar and honey together in a large pan over a low heat, stirring constantly, until the sugar and honey have dissolved. Mix in all the other ingredients. Press the mixture into a lightly greased baking tray and bake at 190°C/375°F/Gas 5 for 15 to 20 minutes, until golden brown. While it is still hot, cut into 16 portions, but leave to cool in the tin, as the flapjack remains soft until it has cooled slightly.

Nutritional information per portion:
Energy 250kcal/1050kJ; Protein 2.5g;
Carbohydrate 34.1g; Fat 11.6g.

Banana bread
Bananas are the classic runner's fuel and this soft loaf should be easy to eat before a run. Adding cinnamon may help control your blood sugar levels, avoiding a crash after the initial burst of energy.

100g/3¼oz/scant 1 cup butter
200g/7oz/1 cup caster (superfine) sugar
2 eggs, beaten
225g/8oz/2 cups wholemeal
*   (whole-wheat) flour*
2.5ml/½ tsp baking powder
5ml/1 tsp cinnamon
200g/7oz ripe bananas, mashed

Cream the butter and sugar together. Beat in the eggs, then fold in the flour, baking powder and cinnamon. Add the bananas and mix thoroughly. Pour the mixture into a greased loaf tin (pan) and bake at 180°C/350°F/Gas 4 for 50 minutes, until risen and golden brown on top (note the consistency of the loaf may remain soft because of the bananas; you can firm it up by refrigerating it later). Slice into ten pieces.

Nutritional information per portion:
Energy 265kcal/1113kJ; Protein 5g;
Carbohydrate 39g; Fat 10.3g.

Natural isotonic drink

This natural isotonic drink delivers the same amount of carbohydrates as a store-bought energy drink – around 6g per 100ml, so it can be absorbed easily on the run. It is very easy to make and cost effective too, as store-bought energy drinks can be expensive. To save time on early-morning runs, make up a bottle the night before and keep chilled in the refrigerator overnight.

Makes 1 litre/1¾ pints/4 cups

500ml/17fl oz/generous 2 cups unsweetened apple juice
500ml/17fl oz/generous 2 cups water
pinch salt

Pour the apple juice and the water into a 1-litre (1¾-pint) sports bottle, then add the pinch of salt. Shake the bottle thoroughly to mix.

Nutritional information per portion Energy 190kcal798kJ; Protein 0.5g; Carbohydrate 55g; Fat 0.5g.

Low-fat fruit loaf

Lack of fat in this loaf makes it easier to digest on the run. It provides enough energy for about an hour of exercise, but be careful of the high fibre content, which could unsettle your stomach.

115g/4oz/1 cup raisins
115g/4oz/1 cup sultanas (golden raisins)
115g/4oz/1 cup currants
25g/1oz/2 tbsp soft dark brown sugar
150ml/¼ pint/⅔ cup hot black tea
10ml/2 tbsp thick-cut marmalade
2 eggs, beaten
175g/6oz/1½ cups wholemeal (whole-wheat) flour
5ml/1 tsp mixed spice (apple pie spice)
30ml/2 tbsp skimmed milk

Soak the fruit and sugar in the tea overnight. Stir in the other ingredients and mix. Pour into a greased and lined loaf tin (pan) and bake at 180°C/350°F/Gas 4 for 1½ hours until firm.

Nutritional information per portion Energy 249kcal/1045kJ; Protein 6.3g; Carbohydrate 50.9g; Fat 2.7g

Above: This fruit loaf has a very low fat content and so is easy for your stomach to digest as you run.

Instant energy

If you don't have the time to spare to make your own training snacks, just grab some natural quick-release energy in the form of:

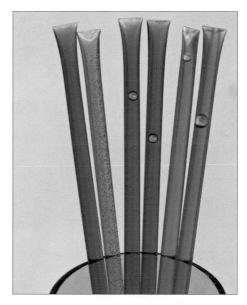

A medium banana: *this will give you enough energy for around 30 minutes of running, as well as potassium to keep your muscles from cramping. Choose very ripe bananas, which are easier to digest.*

Raisins: *this high-energy dried fruit packs a powerful 135kcal/567kJ and 35g of carbohydrates for every 50g (handful). It also contains high levels of antioxidants, which help combat some of the damage done by intense exercise.*

Honey: *clear honey in a squeezy pack (sometimes called a honey stick) makes the perfect natural energy gel. Research suggests it is just as effective as store-bought energy gels for fuelling exercise.*

5K Event: Advanced Schedule

It is a tough distance to get right, but learning how to run 5K to the best of your ability will stand you in good stead for longer distances. It's a great test of speed, stamina and strength of character and is short enough to be raced once a month.

In some ways a 5K road race is more daunting for an experienced runner than for a complete beginner. In training, there are three main areas to work on.

Style

You will need to develop a faster stride for the 5K, especially if you have become used to running farther and slower. Working on your form will help your legs to move quickly and will keep you from wasting energy during the race. Most people find that their style naturally improves when they run a bit faster, but you can work on it. Including regular skills and drills sessions to work on your flexibility, reactions and style will help, as will performing fast strides at the end of some runs.

Below: Working on your running form is important for 5K racing. Include some hill walks and runs in your sessions.

Great athletes: Paavo Nurmi (b. 1897, Turku, Finland, d. 1973)

One of the earliest examples of a strong tradition of Finnish distance runners, Paavo Nurmi won nine Olympic gold medals and three silvers and set countless world

records across a huge spectrum of distances, making him a national hero in his home country. At his first Olympic Games in Antwerp, 1920, he won gold in the 10,000m, two cross-country events, and silver in the 5,000m. He was a determined athlete and his tough training is legendary. He went on to compete at two more Olympics, but in 1932 was not allowed to take part as officials ruled he had accepted too much money for expenses, breaking the strict rules on amateurism. He won his last major race in 1933. In 1952, when the Olympics came to Helsinki, Nurmi carried the torch at the opening ceremony, and there is a statue of him outside the Olympic stadium there.

Left: The Finnish great, Paavo Nurmi, lights the Olympic flame at the 1952 Games in Helsinki.

Pacing

There are two approaches to pacing a 5K. The traditional approach is the negative split – the safer option – where the first half is run slightly slower. However, recent research suggests that the best approach is actually to head out fast and try to hang on. Whichever tactic you choose, you need to develop an instinctive feel for your goal 5K pace, and longer intervals (over 1,000m) can help with this.

Coping with pain

It sounds dramatic, but if you don't feel strong discomfort for at least the last 2km of your 5K race, you are probably not working as hard as you can. Unfortunately it takes practice to learn to deal with this, which is where your mile pace and longer

Right: Running fast intervals of 1,000m and longer is a good way for you to learn pace judgement.

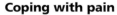

intervals come into play. As you get more experienced you can cut down recovery times between repetitions, which brings you closer to the race experience. For these sessions it is especially useful to train with faster athletes; if you train alone it will be very difficult to force yourself to run this fast for any length of time.

Example six-week schedule

Before starting this schedule, you should be running at least five times a week. Your long run should be at least an hour, and you should be doing one or two speedwork sessions. For longer intervals here (1,000m and beyond) you should aim to run at 3 to 5 seconds faster than a 5K pace; for shorter repetitions aim to run at your mile pace. Speed sessions should include a 10-minute warm-up jog and 10-minute cool-down. Your race goal is faster than 24:30 (8-minute miling); if you are aiming to run sub-20 minutes, reduce the recovery periods between long intervals.

Right: Train with someone slightly faster than you to make sure you push yourself hard enough.

	Mon	Tue	Wed	Thur	Fri	Sat	Sun
5K event: advanced schedule							
Week one	3 easy	2 x 1,000m with 3 min recoveries	5 easy with 4 x 100m strides at end	4 x 800m with 2 min recoveries; 8 x 200m with 200m recoveries	Rest	6km (4 miles) inc. hills	10–13km (6–8 miles)
Week two	4 easy	3 x 1,000m with 3 min recoveries	5 easy with 150m hard, 50m easy x 4 at end	6 x 400m with 90 sec recoveries; 1,200m x 1	Rest	8km (5 miles) inc. hills	13–15km (8–9 miles)
Week three	4 easy	1,000m; 1,600m; 1,000m with 3 min recoveries	4 easy with 6 x 100m strides throughout	6 x 800m with 90 secs–2 mins recoveries	Rest	6km (4 miles) inc. hills	13–16km (8–10 miles)
Week four	4 easy/ cross-train	1,200m, 1,600m, 800m with 3 min recoveries	5 easy with 150m hard, 50m easy x 6	200m, 400m, 800m x 2 with same distance recovery	Rest	6km (4 miles) inc. 10–15 minutes easy fartlek	13–15km (8–9 miles)
Week five	4 easy/ cross-train	1,200m x 3 with 2 min recoveries	5 easy with 4 x 100m strides at end	6 x 400m with 90 secs recoveries; 4 x 200m with same distance recovery	Rest	8km (5 miles) with 6 x 100m strides at end	10–13km (6–8 miles)
Week six	3 easy	3 x 1,000m with 2 min recoveries	Rest/cross-train	6km (4 miles) with 150m hard/50m easy x 4 at end	Rest	3 easy/rests	5K race

10K Event: Advanced Schedule

For the experienced runner, the 10K has a particular draw. It is a fairly short race, so you can recover quickly from it and have several attempts at a personal best over a season, and the nice round 10 kilometres makes it perfect for pace practice.

It is a distance that eludes some of the best professional athletes, but the 10K is worth revisiting several times a year; in the winter as a means of keeping your speed up, and in the summer to ensure you can still cover a decent distance. If you're training for a 5K or for a longer event, then you should be able to run a good 10K time, but if you are training specifically for this distance you'll need to fine-tune your sessions. The key sessions involved in running a 10K are:

Race pace

Some coaches believe that 10K race pace is the most efficient speed for most athletes. However, that is true only if you can get it right. You will use long stretches of 10K pace in your speed sessions to get used to the pace. If you are training for a longer event, the 10K pace will stand you in good stead, as it forms the basis for faster sessions for a half-marathon and longer. If instead you are aiming to knock a huge chunk off your personal best, try these sessions at your current best pace and if they feel easy, step up to your 'dream' pace to see how you cope.

10K event: advanced schedule

	Mon	Tue	Wed	Thur	Fri	Sat	Sun
Week one	Rest	6 x 800m with 400m recoveries	8km (5 miles) with 5 x 100m strides at end	3 x 1.5km (1 mile) at race pace with 4 min recoveries	Rest/ cross-train	8km (5 miles) easy	13–16km (8–10 miles)
Week two	Rest	4 x 200m hard/200 easy; 10 mins easy; 4 x 800m with 400m recoveries	8km (5 miles) easy	1,000m; 1,200m; 1,600m; back down at race pace with 2 min recoveries	Rest/ cross-train	8km (5 miles) easy with 5 x 100m strides	13–16km (8–10 miles)
Week three	Rest	As week 1	6.5km (4 miles) neg split run	4 x 1.5km (1 mile) at race pace with 4 min recoveries	Rest	6.5km (4 miles) easy	16–19km (10–12 miles)
Week four	Rest	As week 2	4km (2.5 miles) neg split run	2 x 1,600m race pace, 4 min recs; then 6 x 200m hard/200m easy	Rest	8km (5 miles) easy	16km (10 miles)
Week five	Rest	6 x 800m (just faster than race pace) with 400m recoveries	8km (5 miles) easy	10K neg split run (on race course if poss.)	Rest/ cross-train	8km (5 miles) easy	13km (8 miles) with 3 x 10 mins 10K pace plus 5 x 100m strides
Week six	Rest	2 x (200m, 400m, 800m, back down); with 200m recoveries	6.5km (4 miles) neg split	5 x 1.5km (1 mile) at race pace with 2 min recoveries	Rest/ cross-train	10km (6 miles) easy	13km (8 miles) with 2 x 10 mins at race pace
Week seven	Rest	As week 5	8km (5 miles) neg split	4 x 1.5km (1 mile) at race pace with 90 sec recoveries	Rest/ cross-train	8km (5 miles) easy	16km (10 miles) easy
Week eight	Rest	6 x 800m, with 400m recoveries	8km (5 miles) neg split	8km (5 miles) easy	Rest	5km (3 miles) easy with 4 x 100m strides	10K race

Great athletes: Haile Gebrselassie (b. 1973, Arsi Province, Ethiopia)

In an international career that began in the early 1990s, Haile Gebrselassie has earned a deserved reputation as one of the greatest distance runners ever. He has set 26 world records, won two Olympic gold medals and four 10,000m golds in four consecutive World Championships.

His first real international breakthrough came at the World Junior Championships in 1992, where he won the 5,000m and 10,000m. He was not without close rivals, mainly fellow African runners, and at the 2000 Olympics in Sydney he beat the Kenyan runner Paul Tergat in the closest 10,000m in Olympic history: the margin was just 0.09 seconds. His next Olympics in Athens was a disappointment; he had hoped to retain his 10,000m title but lost to countryman Kenenisa Bekele. Since that Games,

Left: Haile Gebrselassie running the London Marathon. He set a new world record at the distance in 2008.

Gebrselassie has focused on road races, with impressive wins over 10K, and world records at 10 miles and half-marathon. In 2005, he won all his road races. The one record that seemed to evade him was the marathon. Despite wins at Amsterdam and Berlin, his performances at the Flora London Marathon in 2006 and 2007 ended badly – he pulled out at 18 miles in the latter race. However, later that year, Gebrselassie was vindicated with a new marathon world record, 2:04:26. The following year proved disappointing: having decided not to race the marathon at the Beijing Olympics – he feared the city's pollution would aggravate his asthma – Gebrselassie could only reach sixth place in the 10,000m. He has now turned his attention back to road racing, and broke his own record in 2008, running 2:03:59 in Berlin. He maintains that he will run a marathon in less than 2:03 before the end of his career.

Negative splits

A 10K event is the perfect distance to use the negative split. Practise this in slightly shorter training sessions so that you are able to get used to the feeling of running relaxed then speeding up. Gradually you will build up to a 10K 'time trial', so find a route that is as close as possible to 10K (you can use a track or a treadmill to measure the distance accurately if necessary).

Example eight-week schedule

Before beginning this eight-week schedule you should be running at least five times per week, covering a minimum of 48km (30 miles). You should be able to run for 1 hr 30 mins comfortably, and ideally you will be doing one or two speed sessions per week. All speed sessions should have a 10-minute warm-up jog and 10-minute cool down. Your target race time is 35 to 45 minutes.

Long runs

It may seem strange to run almost to half-marathon distance during a 10K schedule, but without this comfortable

Right: Some coaches believe that 10K pace is the most efficient speed.

level of endurance you won't be able to sustain a fast pace. It's also worth bearing in mind that the 10K can be the stepping stone to great

marathons – as it has been for many an elite athlete, such as the great Gebrselassie – so you won't regret maintaining your long-run base.

Half-marathon: Advanced Schedule

Half-marathon training is not dissimilar to training for the full distance, and most runners train for both concurrently. The noticeable difference is in the pace, which, if you are racing well, should be considerably less relaxed than at marathon level.

Half-marathons tend to be run just below lactate threshold pace, so you need to practise this more often in training. You can only estimate your exact lactate threshold without being tested, but for most people it is around 80 to 85 per cent of their maximum heart rate. Some of your sessions will be longer runs with periods of threshold and race pace running built in.

The mileage needed for a half-marathon almost matches that of a marathon schedule. You can run a half-marathon with fewer really long runs, but to be able to push the pace you will need to be comfortable over much longer distances. In fact, if you have

Below: Over 24,000 participants competed in the 28th Berlin half-marathon in April 2008.

time to build up to running twice a day, then you should add an extra 30 to 40 minute easy run to every day (separate from the sessions listed on the plan).

Example 12-week plan
To follow this plan you must have been running five or six times a week for several months, with one long run of 1hr 30 mins and two speed sessions per week. For intervals over a mile (5 to 8 minutes) in length, run at threshold or race pace; for one-mile repetitions use 10K pace; for 400 to 800m use 5K pace. Each speedwork and threshold session should begin with a 10-minute warm-up.

Left: To run a fast half-marathon, your mileage will need to almost equal full marathon training.

Half-marathon: advanced schedule

	Mon	Tue	Wed	Thur	Fri	Sat	Sun
Week one	5km (3 miles) easy/cross-train	6 x 800m with 400m recoveries	8km (5 miles) easy with 5 x 100m strides throughout	2 x 10 mins threshold, 5 mins recovery	8km (5 miles) easy	Rest/ cross-train	16–19km (10–12 miles)
Week two	5km (3 miles) easy/cross-train	400m, 800m, 1,200m, 1,600m then back with 400m recoveries	8km (5 miles) easy with 5 x 100m strides throughout	15 mins threshold; 10 mins recovery then 5 x 200m fast but relaxed	8km (5 miles) easy	Rest/ cross-train	19–22km (12–14 miles)
Week three	5km (3 miles) easy/cross-train	8 x 800m with 400m recoveries	10km (6 miles) easy with 5 x 100m strides throughout	15 mins threshold; 10 mins recovery then 5 x 200m fast but relaxed	8km (5 miles) easy	Rest/ cross-train	22–25km (14–16 miles) with 2 x 10 mins at race pace
Week four	8km (5 miles) easy/cross-train	4 x 1 mile with 2–3 min recoveries	10km (6 miles) easy with 8 x 100m strides throughout	3 x 10 mins threshold; 5 min recoveries	10km (6 miles) easy	Rest/ cross-train	26–29km (16–18 miles) with 3 x 10 mins at race pace
Week five	8km (5 miles) easy/cross-train	8 x 800m with 400m recoveries	10km (6 miles) easy with 8 x 100m strides throughout	2 x 15 mins threshold with 5 mins recovery	10km (6 miles) easy	Rest/ cross-train	32km (20 miles) with 2 x 20 mins at race pace
Week six	Cross-train/rest	2 x 800m, 1,600m, 2,000m with 3 min recoveries	10km (6 miles) easy with 5 x 200m fast but relaxed	2 x 15 mins threshold with 5 mins recovery	10km (6 miles) easy	Rest/ cross-train	22–25km (14–16 miles) with 3 x 15 mins at race pace; or race 10K
Week seven	8km (5 miles) easy/cross-train	2 x 800m, 1,600m, 2,000m with 3 min recoveries	10km (6 miles) easy with 5 x 200m fast but relaxed	30 mins threshold	10km (6 miles) easy	Rest/ cross-train	32km (20 miles) with 40 mins at race pace
Week eight	5km (3 miles) easy/cross-train	5 x 1 mile with 2–3 min recoveries then 5 x 150m fast/50m easy	6.5km (4 miles) easy	30 mins threshold	10km (6 miles) easy	Rest/ cross-train	29km (18 miles) with 3 x 15 mins at race pace
Week nine	8km (5 miles) easy/cross-train	10 x 800m with 400m recoveries	10km (6 miles) easy with 8 x 100m strides	2 x 20 mins threshold with 5 mins recovery	10km (6 miles) easy	Rest/ cross-train	22–25km (14–16 miles) with 2 x 20 mins at race pace; or race 10K
Week ten	8km (5 miles) easy/cross-train	5 x 1 mile with 2–3 min recoveries then 5 x 150m fast/50m easy	10km (6 miles) easy; gradually accelerate over last 2 miles	30 mins threshold	10km (6 miles) easy	Rest/ cross-train	22–25km (14–16 miles) with 2 x 20 mins at race pace
Week eleven	8km (5 miles) easy/cross-train	6 x 800m with 400m recoveries	8km (5 miles) easy with 8 x 100m strides	2 x 15 mins threshold with 5 min recovery; 5 x 200m fast but relaxed	10km (6 miles) easy	Rest/ cross-train	16km (10 miles) easy
Week twelve	5km (3 miles) easy/cross-train	Rest	Rest/cross-train	5 miles easy	Rest	5km (3 miles) easy with 5 x 100m strides	Half-marathon

Marathon: Elite Schedule

The traditional and most widely accepted method of marathon training is to run a high mileage, six or seven days a week, reaching more than 160 kilometres or 100 miles per week in training. This training is not just the preserve of top marathon runners.

Running an elite schedule is hard on your body and should not be attempted unless you have gradually built up a base fitness for this distance. However, if you can handle it, you will be using a similar schedule to the world's best marathon runners.

The key sessions for this schedule are similar to other approaches, but it requires running twice a day from Monday to Friday, with a second semi-long run halfway through the week. Your long runs are also slightly longer, reaching 37–38km (23–24 miles) at their peak.

The 12-week schedule

The easy runs are not listed in the table as they remain constant throughout: run 6–10km (4–6 miles) each morning from Monday to Friday. Remember to

Right: Following a high-mileage schedule is tough but is the surest way to reach the front of the pack.

Great athletes: Paula Radcliffe (b. 1973, Davenham, Cheshire, UK)

In the early stages of Paula Radcliffe's career, it seemed that she would be another young athlete full of never-realized potential. She broke into elite running in 1992 with a convincing win in the junior race at the World Cross-country Championships. However, a series of injuries, illnesses and – many thought – a weak sprint finish left her out of the medals in track races at major competitions. Radcliffe finally found her distance in 2002 when she ran the fastest ever debut marathon, winning the London race in 2:18:56, a women-only record. She went on to break the women's world record in Chicago later that year, then took her time down again to 2:15:25 at the 2003 Flora London Marathon.

Left: Paula Radcliffe after winning the New York City Marathon in 2007, pictured with second-placed Gete Wami.

The following year saw the lowest point of her career to date, when exhaustion and injury caused her to pull out of the Olympic marathon in Athens, where she was favourite to win. There was some consolation that autumn when she won the New York City Marathon in a sprint finish against Susan Chepkemei, and then in 2005 when she won gold in the marathon at the World Championships in Helsinki. Radcliffe took time off in 2006 and most of 2007, when she had her first child. Following victory in the New York City Marathon in November 2007, more disappointment followed when her training for the Beijing Olympics was ruined by a stress fracture; determined to finish the marathon, she struggled home in 23rd place. However, she is still aiming for an Olympic gold medal before she retires.

Marathon: elite schedule

	Mon	Tue	Wed	Thur	Fri	Sat	Sun
Week one	10km (6 miles)	8 x 800m with 400m recoveries	10–13km (6–8 miles)	2 x 10 min threshold, 5 mins recovery	10km (6 miles) with 6 x 3 mins hill reps	6km (4 miles)/ rest	19–22km (12–14 miles)
Week two	10km (6 miles)	800m, 1,200m, 1,600m then back with 400m recoveries	13–16km (8–10 miles)	2 x 10 min threshold, 5 mins recovery	10km (6 miles) with 6 x 3 mins hill reps	6km (4 miles)/ rest	19–22km (12–14 miles)
Week three	10km (6 miles)	8 x 800m with 400m recoveries	13–16km (8–10 miles)	2 x 15 min threshold, 5 mins recovery	10km (6 miles) with 6 x 3 mins hill reps	6km (4miles)/ rest	22–26km (14–16 miles)
Week four	10km (6 miles)	5 x 1 mile with 2–3 min recoveries	10–13km (6–8 miles)	1 x 15 mins threshold	10km (6 miles) with 5 x 100m strides	6km (4 miles)/ rest	26–29km (16–18 miles)
Week five	10km (6 miles)	10 x 800m with 400m recoveries	16–19km (10–12 miles)	2 x 15 min threshold, 5 mins recovery	10km (6 miles) with 8 x 3 mins hill reps	10km (6 miles)/ rest	32km (20 miles)
Week six	10km (6 miles)	2 x 800m, 1,600m, 2,000m with 3 min recoveries	16–19km (10–12 miles)	25 mins threshold	10km (6 miles) negative split run	10km (6 miles) rest	35km (22 miles)
Week seven	10km (6 miles)	2 x 400m, 800m, 1,200m with 3 min recoveries	19–22km (12–14 miles)	30 mins threshold	10km (6 miles) fartlek session	10km (6 miles) rest	29km (18 miles)
Week eight	10km (6 miles)	5 x 1 mile with 2–3 min recoveries then 5 x 150m fast/50m easy	19–22km (12–14 miles)	30 mins threshold	10km (6 miles) with 4 x 5 mins hill reps	10km (6 miles)/ rest	35–38km (22–24 miles)
Week nine	10km (6 miles)	8 x 800m with 400m recoveries	19–22km (12–14 miles)	35 mins threshold	10km (6 miles) with 6 x 3 mins hill reps	10km (6 miles)/rest	29km (18 miles)
Week ten	10km (6 miles)	3 x 1 mile with 2–3 min recoveries then 5 x 150m fast/50m easy	16–19km (10–12 miles)	20 mins threshold	6km (4 miles) negative split run	10km (6 miles)/ rest	26km (16 miles)
Week eleven	10km (6 miles)	6 x 800m with 400m recoveries	10–13km (6–8 miles)	20 mins threshold	6km (4 miles) fartlek session	10km (6 miles)/ rest	19km (12 miles)
Week twelve	5km (3 miles)	Rest/cross-train	5km (3 miles)	Rest/cross-train	Rest	5km (3 miles) easy/rest	Marathon

run two miles as a warm-up and cool-down for all speed and threshold sessions. You'll notice that there is the option to run every single day with this plan, but you should only run the Saturday session if you feel really strong and full of energy. Many elite runners will train every day but it takes years of conditioning to cope with this, so if you want to play it safe, stick with six days' training per week.

Try to run some of your longer efforts at race pace – perhaps just 40 to 50 minutes in the middle – to get used to how it feels. Also, if you have time, add two weight training sessions per week (on easy run days), and two Pilates sessions to maintain core strength – the higher your mileage, the more important this is to help you avoid injury.

Marathon Training the Easy Way

Logging hundreds of miles might be the best way to train for a front-of-race marathon performance, but it doesn't suit everyone. The good news is that for the average runner, great results are possible from running just three times a week, if you make the sessions count.

If you find that your training is always interrupted by impact-related injuries, or family and work commitments mean you simply don't have time to run 160km (100 miles) per week, then you can still run a good marathon with just three running sessions per week. In fact, for a marathon runner with a few years' experience, this type of training plan can bring the kind of results that win smaller races.

Sometimes high-mileage training programmes are criticized for containing too many junk miles – easy, aimless running which, some would argue, simply put you at higher risk of overtraining or picking up an injury. The key with lower-mileage training is to make sure that every run you do really counts. Your three runs per

Below: Hill training and other quality training sessions build your strength and speed without injury risk.

Low-mileage training tested

It takes a leap of faith for any marathon runner to cut down to three runs a week, but science is on your side. In 2003, a group of scientists and runners at Furman University, South Carolina, USA, formed the Furman Institute of Running and Science Training (FIRST). They trained a group of 25 volunteers using a rigid three-runs-per-week schedule. Of the 21 runners who finished the target marathon, 15 ran personal bests. Laboratory tests showed that their oxygen uptake had gone up by 4.2 per cent, their lactate threshold speed had increased by 2.3 per cent, and their body fat had gone down by an average of 8.7 per cent. For further details of their programme visit their website at www.furman.edu/FIRST.

Above: In this type of schedule, your long runs should be quite fast – at target marathon pace.

week are a speed run, a tempo or hill run, and a long run. In addition to the three runs per week, you should aim to cross-train for two sessions a week to keep your fitness levels high and weight down. Some runners even find that they gain fitness using this method; you can train harder on your cross-training days than you would running, as the change of activity uses different muscles and usually has no impact, so your running muscles get the rest they need. Your overall fitness should improve, your body fat should reduce (making you a more efficient runner), and your risk of injury should be lower, putting you in great shape to tackle the marathon.

Marathon: easy schedule

	Day one	Day two	Day three	Day four	Day five
Week one	6 x 800m with 400m recoveries	Cross-train 30 mins	2 x 20 mins tempo with 5 mins recovery	Cross-train 30 mins	16–19km (10–12 miles)
Week two	3 x 1,600m with 3–4 min recoveries	Cross-train 30 mins	5 miles with 6 x 2 mins uphill effort	Cross-train 30 mins	19–22km (12–14 miles)
Week three	3 x (400m, 800m) with 400m recoveries	Cross-train 40 mins	40 mins tempo run	Cross-train 40 mins	22–26km (14–16 miles)
Week four	6 x 800m with 400m recoveries	Cross-train 30 mins	40 mins tempo run	Cross-train 30 mins	16–19km (10–12 miles)
Week five	4 x 1,200m with 600m recoveries, then 4 x 400m with 200m recoveries	Cross-train 40 mins	5 miles with total 10–15 mins uphill effort	Cross-train 40 mins	26–29km (16–18 miles)
Week six	8 x 800m	Cross-train 40 mins	50 mins tempo run	Cross-train 40 mins	29–32km (18–20 miles)
Week seven	4 x 1,600m with 3 min recoveries	Cross-train 45 mins	1hr tempo run	Cross-train 45 mins	32km (20 miles)
Week eight	4 x 1,200m with 600m recoveries	Cross-train 45 mins	5 miles with 4 x 2 mins uphill effort	Cross-train 45 mins	19km (12 miles)
Week nine	10 x 800m	Cross-train 45 mins	1hr 10 mins tempo run	Cross-train 45 mins	29km (18 miles)
Week ten	4 x 1,400m with 600m recoveries, then 4 x 400m with 200m recoveries	Cross-train 40 mins	1hr 10 mins tempo run	Cross-train 40 mins	26km (16 miles)
Week eleven	6 x 800m	Cross-train 40 mins	50 mins tempo run	Cross-train 40 mins	16–19km (10–12 miles)
Week twelve	Rest	Cross-train 30 mins	5km (3 miles) easy/ easy cross-train	Cross-train 30 mins/rest	Marathon

The 12-week schedule

There are only three runs a week in this schedule, but you must complete them all (if you like you can add a fourth easy run) and you must put effort in. On your long runs, stay close to your target marathon pace, even adding bursts of half-marathon pace running. Do your tempo runs at 10K pace (just faster than threshold pace), long intervals (1,000 to 1,600m) at 5K pace and 800m or less at mile pace. Choose an activity you enjoy for your cross-training and treat your cross-training sessions as high-quality workouts, adding faster intervals and higher resistance for extra fitness gains. Scientists (see box opposite) have found that runners can see much greater improvements in marathon times when they take the cross-training sessions as seriously as they would a speed workout or long run, so decide before each session what kind of training you will do and make the sessions progressively harder as the weeks go by.

Right: You can cross-train hard once or twice a week, building fitness and reducing body fat.

Marathon: Heart-rate Training

It can be difficult to tell how hard you are training, as your mood, the weather and even illness all have an effect on your perception of effort. What's more, until you are experienced at racing over a range of distances, it can also be hard to judge your pace.

Above: When you first begin heart-rate training, you may find it frustrating running slower than usual.

be able to stay below your lactate threshold, which in turn means you are less likely to hit the wall.

Finding your target zones

You can choose to have laboratory tests to find your different heart-rate training zones, but if you don't have the time or money for that, use these simple sums.

First of all, you need to find out your maximum heart rate (MHR). You can do this using the formula 214 – (0.8 x age) for men, or 209 – (0.9 x age) for women. For a more accurate figure, however, use this test (which you should not attempt if you are very unfit or new to exercise): warm up, then run for 4 minutes as fast as you can on a treadmill; take a 2-minute recovery jog, then repeat the hard run. You should hit your MHR toward the end of your second fast interval.

Below: A basic heart-rate monitor is enough to tell you when you're in the right training zone.

This is where introducing objective science, in the form of heart-rate training, can be useful. Switching to heart-rate training can be frustrating for runners used to pushing themselves as hard as they can. Running at your target heart rate feels incredibly slow at first. Your body – and your willpower – allow you to train much harder than is beneficial, often leading to overtraining or injury. To begin heart-rate training from scratch, you will need to spend a period building a base, training at less than 60 per cent of your working heart rate (WHR, see below) and excluding speedwork. You will gradually be able to run faster at the same heart rate, and after this you can add speedwork and tempo runs. The advantage of training this way is that your heart rate should be lower in marathons, so you should

Find your resting heart rate (RHR) by wearing the heart-rate monitor to bed. In the morning it will tell you the minimum heart rate achieved during sleep.

Work out your WHR like this:
1 MHR – RHR = x
(for example 205 – 44 = 161)
2 Take the effort level you need to achieve, say 60 per cent, and multiply this by your WHR
(for example 161 x 0.6 = 97)

Left: Once you've found your working heart rate, use it to plan sessions.

3 Add this figure to your RHR to find your target heart rate
(for example 97 + 44 = 141 bpm).

Applying zones to training: 12-week schedule
Follow this schedule after building up your base using a heart-rate monitor. You can use the alarm on your monitor to tell you when you have hit your target rate. Figures are percentage WHR. Before and after each speed session (Days Two and Four) do 10 minutes at 60 per cent WHR.

Marathon: heart-rate training

	Day one	Day two	Day three	Day four	Day five
Week one	40 mins at 60%	5 mins at 70%; 4 mins at 85%; 3 mins at 85–90%; then run all-out for 1 min; then back down	40 mins fartlek at 70%	2 x 10 mins at 80% with 3 mins recovery	1:30 at 60–70%
Week two	40 mins at 60%	2 x 10 mins at 85–90%, recovering to 55% in between	40 mins fartlek at 70–85%	15 mins at 80%	1:45 at 60–70%
Week three	40 mins at 60%	As week 1	40 mins fartlek at 70–85%	3 x 8 mins at 80% with 3 mins recovery	2:00 at 60–70%
Week four	40 mins at 60%	3 x 5 mins at 85–90%, recovering to 55% in between	50 mins fartlek at 70–85%	20 mins at 80%	2:15 at 60–70%
Week five	40 mins at 60%	As week 1, but repeat sequence	50 mins fartlek at 70–85%	25 mins at 80%	2:30 at 60–70%
Week six	40 mins at 60%	8 x run up to 90%, recover to 55%	1 hour fartlek at 70–85%	30 mins at 80%	3:00 at 60–70%
Week seven	40 mins at 60%	4 x 4 mins at 85–90%, recovering to 55% in between	40 mins fartlek at 70–85%	20 mins at 80%	2:30 at 60–70%
Week eight	40 mins at 60%	As week 5	1 hour fartlek at 70–85%	35 mins at 80%	3:00 at 60–70%
Week nine	40 mins at 60%	10 x run up to 90%, recovering to 55%	1 hour fartlek at 70–85%	40 mins at 80%	2:45 at 60–70%
Week ten	40 mins at 60%	6 x 4 mins at 85–90%, recovering to 55%	50 mins fartlek at 70–85%	40 mins at 80%	2:30 at 60–70%
Week eleven	40 mins at 60%	As week 1	40 mins fartlek at 70–85%	20 mins at 80%	1:45 at 60–70%
Week twelve	40 mins at 60%	Rest	30 mins fartlek at 70–85%	Rest	Marathon

Key Race-training Sessions

Every workout you do helps you to reach the start line of your race in peak condition. But just as specific running training is the only way to become a better runner, putting in a few race-specific sessions is the best way to be competitive on the big day.

Race training sessions are not the same as speedwork; though many are fast, the point of these workouts is always to replicate race-day conditions in some way. The following workouts will help you feel confident and ready to race.

Race-day warm-up

You'll need a thorough warm-up before your race, and you should practise this before some of your training sessions. Run gently for 5 minutes. Then, find some flat, even, soft ground and do 20–30m (65–98ft) of high knees (skipping

Below: Group fartlek sessions, where you take it in turns to dictate pace, are great race practice.

forward, on the balls of your feet, kicking your knees high in front); cover the same distance with some heel kicks ('running' forward kicking your heels right back to your bottom). Use your arms throughout, pumping them back and forward. Finish the warm-up with a few more minutes' light running.

Race pace practice

Even if you've chosen to do most of your long runs at a slow pace, you should add a couple of race-pace sections during the hardest point of your training (usually 6–8 weeks before the race). Work out your mile pace based on your target race time, but be flexible – if you can't talk after 30–40 minutes at this pace in training, or if your heart rate

is consistently above 85 per cent MHR, it's too fast (if you're aiming for a marathon or half, your race pace should feel very comfortable over a short distance). You can find your ideal training pace, and work out a predicted race pace, using the tables at the end of the book.

At the sharp end of a race, there are likely to be several surges in pace as different people try to establish a lead. Sometimes people may even deliberately slow the pace, which can be off-putting (and is meant to be!). Learn to cope with this using group fartlek sessions. Gather a group of friends of different paces and abilities, and draw numbers out of a hat. Don't tell anyone else which number you have. After 10 minutes of easy

Above: It's impossible to know how you'll feel on race day but visualizing the event will help.

jogging, the person with number one goes to the lead, running as fast as they like for any length of time from 1 to 5 minutes, then shouts "End!" The group jogs to recover and regroup for 2 or 3 minutes, then the next person takes the lead without warning; and so on until everyone in the group has led an interval.

Negative split

This is by far the safest approach to pacing long events (10K or more), so it makes sense to practise it in training (it features strongly in our 10K Schedules). The simplest way to do this is to find a short, fairly straight out-and-back route and run the return leg faster, but remember you're aiming for a very close split, so don't crawl the first half and sprint the second. Go for a time that is just a minute or two faster over the second leg.

Right: Try running hard at the end of sessions, when you're already tired, to toughen yourself up.

Fast finish

Even if you're not a naturally fast finisher, you can train to develop a good final kick, which will often put you at an advantage, especially in races of 10K or less. Short, sharp speed sessions will develop the basic leg speed you need for this, but you should also try sprinting when you're already tired. At the end of a threshold or race-pace section, without a recovery break, accelerate smoothly into a 200m sprint. Recover for 30 seconds, then repeat. Build up to three or four sprints over a few weeks.

Dress rehearsal

Try to visit your race course before race day. If you can, have a run out over the course the week before, practising your pace and fuelling strategy (but relaxing toward the end of the route). If you can't get to your course, then choose a route with similar characteristics (e.g. gradient and surface), and run it at the same time of day as your race will be.

Races are perhaps the best kind of specific race training you can do. Up to 16km (10 miles), you can even race the same distance in your build-up, but treat it as a practice run so you don't wear yourself out. For the marathon or half, shorter races are a good progress check and help you to cope with race-day nerves, practise your warm-up and nutrition strategies, and even find out which kit you're most comfortable in.

Above: When you're running well, hold on to the feeling for race day.

Try to set aside some time in the few weeks before your race to think through your race day and visualize everything going according to plan, right up to crossing the line in your target time. You can also use training sessions: when you feel you're running smoothly and strongly, tell yourself 'I will run this well on race day.'

Race Tactics

You might think race tactics are only for athletes at the very front of a race, but a little planning is useful for anyone hoping to perform well. Well-rehearsed tactics can shave seconds off your time or just boost your confidence with a higher placing.

The most important decision you will have to make is how to pace your race. Confident and well-trained runners run as evenly as they can. However this is a difficult approach to take, as other runners will try to influence your pace. Runners who have a strong sprint finish will try to hold the pace slow to keep something for the end of the race, while those who don't have this strength may force the pace early on to create a gap between themselves and the rest of the field. Paula Radcliffe uses this tactic to good effect in most of her marathons. Forcing surges in pace also exhausts sprint finishers, so they are unable to use their end kick.

Assessing the competition

Your choice of pacing strategy may depend on who else is running. If you are at the sharp end of a race and know some of the other fast athletes, try to discover who are the main threats beforehand, working out what kind of runners they are, what times they have run recently, and how they are likely to respond to your tactics.

You can use other runners to help you through your race, particularly in longer road events. Psychologically it is difficult to run alone for long periods of time: you will become too focused on your own discomfort and may lose perspective and find it difficult to judge your pace. Staying with a group of runners means you can use them as pacers, and you can use them either to distract yourself (perhaps by chatting as you run if they are willing and able to talk), or to help focus you on the race pace. You can also draft behind groups of runners, effectively using them as a windblock to minimize resistance to your own forward motion. For this to work, you need to stay close behind the other runners.

Above: You can use the other runners taking part to help you stick to your pace in crowded events.

Using earphones

Earphones have become an increasingly common feature at long-distance road events, and it is true that music can be useful to help keep you on pace as you run. However, the running community is divided over whether they should be allowed at large events, some feeling that it is rude and anti-social to wear them, others arguing that it is simply a safety issue. If you choose to run wearing your earphones, don't put them on until you have started so that you don't miss any announcements. Keep the volume low enough so that you can hear someone if they are trying to get your attention.

Above: Take it in turns to lead a pack of runners, as it's harder to run at the front all the way.

Crowd control

Ensure the crowd doesn't work against you. Don't waste energy weaving in and out of others to move forward – run to the outside and sprint around the group. Water stations are prime spots for losing places, so be prepared. If possible, have your friends and family hand out drinks to you slightly apart from the official water station, so you don't end up in a scrummage, and have your water in bottles rather than cups. Also, don't be pushed into running on the outside of a group, as courses are measured along the shortest route possible (in big races this is sometimes marked by a line painted on the road).

Whatever your race plan, it will be effective only if you stick to it. Don't allow yourself to be distracted by others' tactics – after all, this may be precisely what they are relying on to gain an advantage.

Below: Be courteous to runners around you and if you need to change pace, warn them by calling out.

Below: Over longer distances your race tactics may not come into play until the final few miles.

Mental Training: Long-distance Strategies

Any sports event requires as much mental strength as physical fitness, but the mind plays a far greater role for long-distance runners. In a marathon, whether a first-timer or about to set a world record, your body will be aching and your instincts telling you to stop.

The last few miles in any long-distance event are extremely gruelling. At this point, the only thing that will keep you going is a strong mind.

Disassociation vs focusing

There are two main approaches to getting through long-distance events. The first, disassociation, is where the athlete tries to distract himself from the discomfort, fatigue and sometimes boredom of the race. For recreational runners, listening to music while racing is a good example of this (some experts also believe that music can help you run

faster). Other techniques might be playing mental games – trying to remember a list of past winners of the race, or something completely unrelated such as your top ten favourite films.

Focusing is the opposite approach, and is tough to do in a marathon – it takes practice. With this approach, you concentrate intently on the task in hand. Be careful not to focus on the negative (aches and pains, loss of confidence) and instead focus on your breathing, your style, and the feel of the pace. Think about all the training you have put in and the goal you have for the race.

Below: Focusing on the positive, perhaps by remembering good training sessions, helps to keep you strong.

Left: Some scientists believe that listening to music while you run can actually make you faster.

Above: When you are competing in a race, learn to focus on your tactics and competitors to stay on target.

If you are at the competitive end of the race, think about your tactics and the opponents around you. Research has shown that the focusing approach is more successful, so it is worth practising, however unpleasant – try it in shorter races first.

Motivation

To train for a long race, you will have had strong motivation. Keep that in mind as you race. Remind yourself what you want to get from it, whether it is a specific time, to beat a particular opponent, or to win. Studies have shown that people who race for intrinsic rewards (to feel good about themselves, to achieve a new personal best) are more successful than those who compete for extrinsic rewards (their coach's approval, prize money). Whatever your goal was, it should be strong enough to push you to the finish when the going gets tough.

Visualization

This technique is widely used by elite athletes and can be applied to your life in general. The idea is to visualize running a successful race over and over again and in as much detail as possible. Think about your smooth, strong running style, hitting each mile bang on target pace, and finishing strongly and in your desired time. Just thinking about these actions produces the same effect on your brain as if you had actually done them, and so creates a pattern of success. Practise visualization two or three times a day, in a quiet, calm space, and run through your success just before your race and when you hit bad patches.

Enjoyment

Toward the end of your race, it is easy to feel tired and grumpy, particularly if you have missed a mile time by 30 seconds and start to believe you are failing. Try to focus on your enjoyment of the sport: appreciate the strengths of your body and the success you have had in training. Try not to count down the miles; if it helps, slip into your race pace, trust yourself to stay on target by intuition, and promise yourself not to look at your watch for three or four miles.

Mental Training: Winning Strategies

In any race, at any distance, it could be argued that essentially, winning comes down to mental toughness. Two competing athletes who have exactly the same ability and training must use all their mental powers to gain victory.

The elite athlete is often portrayed as an aggressive opponent, 'destroying' other competitors, but there is far more to winning than fighting talk, and whether you are aiming to win or just to perform to your very best, these strategies can help you.

Toughness
Mental toughness is an important quality for endurance runners in particular, but there is a great deal of debate over whether runners are born with it or learn it. The truth is probably somewhere in between. You can help yourself to become mentally strong by using 'character building' workouts: run at race pace in training, pit yourself against faster athletes, train in difficult

Below: Try to think like a winner, no matter what your speed, to help you to achieve your goals.

conditions. Coaches will sometimes teach their athletes to cope with stress by arranging for interruptions to training, or changing plans at the last minute. This helps runners deal with unexpected problems and stay focused on their race.

Self-confidence
There is a fine line between self-confidence and unfounded arrogance, but it is an important distinction: the latter will lead to complacency, disappointment and ultimately loss of confidence. Self-confidence is crucial, however, as positive 'self-talk' is a valuable tool in helping you to maintain your pace through rough patches in a race. Use affirmations in training that you can call on again on race day – say out loud, 'I am strong', 'I can achieve my target', or train yourself out of weaknesses (for example 'I will run smoothly' if you know you have a problem with erratic style).

Above: Sprinters are known for their focus, but relaxation techniques will help runners over any distance.

You can also build up your confidence by thinking about past successes, by going through your training diary to reassure yourself that you have done all you can, and by asking other people (such as your coach or training partners) what they feel are your strengths.

Focus
Watch top-class sprinters before a 100m race, and you will see them go through their own rituals to help them focus on the task ahead. Focus and 'getting in the zone' is also crucial for longer-distance runners. You need to calm any pre-race nerves without becoming so calm that you breeze through the race without putting full effort into it. Relaxation techniques such as deep breathing, or energizing techniques such

Left: If a race is going to be physically tough, you will also need to be mentally tough and should train for this.

can do to prevent it from happening again, and move on. Otherwise the memory of your disappointing race will spoil future performances.

Analyse your performances
If you have a coach, he will be able to give you feedback, but it is also useful to become more self-aware so that you're constantly assessing your own strengths and weaknesses. Sports psychologists sometimes teach athletes to use a technique known as performance profiling. The runner draws up of a list of traits they think are important in their sport (for example relaxation, focus, enjoyment); rates the relative importance of each trait for a 'perfect' athlete; and then rates their own performance for each of the attributes. This is a good way of objectifying yourself to determine which areas you need to work on.

as thinking intently about your target or an opponent, can be useful in achieving the right balance.

Think like a winner
You may have heard gold medallists saying that if they didn't think they would win, they wouldn't race. You may not

Below: Events with different elements, such as triathlon or adventure racing, require renewed focus for each stage

expect to come first, but you can adopt this approach. Instead of heading to a race and thinking 'I'll see what happens' or 'I'll do my best', be determined to achieve your target time or the position you want. Do not allow doubt to take over your mind at any time. However, if your race does not go to plan, don't waste time punishing yourself. The best athletes make mistakes sometimes, and sometimes conditions are against them. Work out what went wrong, what you

Below: Your training partner can build your confidence by reminding you of your strengths.

Advanced Racing Kit

At the start of any running race, it is clear which people are going to be the front runners. The difference can be seen not just in their lean, muscular physiques, but also in the pared-down clothing they wear.

Choosing special kit for a race may not take much off your finish time, but it could give you an extra edge. Light, comfortable kit should be barely noticeable, enabling you to fully focus on the clock and your opponents as you run. Wearing the right kit is about more than the science of running faster, however: racing kit should make you feel confident, strong and psyched up, and this psychological benefit will be more noticeable to you than any reduction in weight or drag.

If you buy special kit for a race, make sure that you have worn it beforehand (especially your shoes); this is not the time to test new styles, as something as seemingly innocuous as a badly placed seam could chafe and ruin a good run. At the opposite end of the spectrum, if you have been wearing the same

Left: Cross-country and track spikes are light with little cushioning and breathable uppers.

Below: Use a spanner to remove the spikes.

Right: As the name suggests, the shoes have removable spikes that add traction.

'lucky' T-shirt for five years, perhaps it is time to treat yourself to something better suited.

Performance shoes
Most shoe manufacturers now make a range of shoes especially designed for fast training and racing. These typically weigh less than 300g (for a men's UK size 8/US size 9), and have been stripped of most of the technical features found in standard training shoes. They have less cushioning, fit more snugly, and may have a more curved shape for faster running.

Heavy runners or those with serious gait problems should avoid these shoes. For track and cross-country races, you can wear 'spikes' or 'racing flats', which look like old-fashioned running slippers. As the name suggests, some have spikes that screw into the outer sole for better traction on the ground.

Left: Good technical kit can give you a powerful psychological edge when it comes to your race day.

Above: These track shoes have shorter spikes and are made for middle-distance running.

Shorts and tights

In a race situation, you want to carry as little weight and bulk as possible, so many people go for traditional, very short, vented shorts, which allow your legs a fuller range of movement (although they are not for the self-conscious!). Tight shorts are another good option as they minimize the risk of chafing on the insides of your legs. In winter, it is worth wearing full-length tights to keep your muscles warm and to avoid cramp. Whichever you choose, unless you are on a very long race, keep pockets to a minimum – you need only a small internal key pocket.

Tops

Fast runners tend to opt for sleeveless tops, but be careful that the armholes don't chafe. Sleeveless tops not only reduce the weight of your outfit but keep you cool, which is essential at the front-end of a race. Loose-weave tops are a good choice as you will need to use safety pins to attach your race number.

It is not really worth wearing a jacket to a race, even on a cold day. It is very difficult to pin your number to it, it becomes too hot after a few minutes' running, and the extra bulk can slow you down. If the weather is poor, stay inside as long as possible before the start or wear a bin-liner (trash bag), which you can throw away once you get going Make sure you have some warm clothes to put on straight after the race.

Compression kit

This is a fairly new phenomenon in sportswear, but one which has quickly become popular. Compression kit is always very tight, and some types have plastic webbing to support muscles. Originating in team sports and power sports (such as sprinting), the idea behind this kit (worn as a base layer) is that it increases bloodflow and therefore oxygen delivery to your working muscles. As such, it is also said to help with recovery. The best compression kit has graded pressure to help keep blood circulating. Research suggests that good compression kit is genuinely effective at improving endurance and aiding recovery, but it is more likely to give an edge to a good athlete than to transform an average runner. In fact, one of its biggest selling points is that it gives you a psychological boost by making you more aware of your muscles.

Left: Compression kit is very tight to support the muscles.

Above: Traditional racing vests are the lightest, coolest option and will keep you comfortable.

Left: Tight shorts minimize chafing – these trail shorts also have handy loops to hold energy gels.

Above: Compression kit boosts bloodflow to your muscles and makes you aware of your body.

Advanced Equipment

While top-end apparel and shoes are essential for fast racing, investing in some essential equipment will give your training an edge – and having splashed out a week's wages to buy a new watch, you will certainly feel motivated to use it.

Once you've started measuring your training it's easy to find plenty of gadgets to help you out, from simple stopwatches to the most advanced GPS speed and distance monitors.

Watches

Time is very much of the essence for runners. The more you run, the more detail you will want to know – which is why that old plastic watch you have had since you were 12 will no longer be good enough. Sports watches can have a bewildering array of functions, but the ones you need to look out for are:

Chronograph. The chronograph or stopwatch mode is the most basic requirement for a sports watch. Most will be capable of recording far longer times than you will ever be running in one go, but make sure the display is detailed enough: if you enjoy doing fast sprints on the track, you will want to know your time down to hundredths of a second.

Lap timer. Recording your lap times or mile splits is a useful way of tracking your progress and training yourself to pace runs evenly. Some watches store up to 300 split times, which sounds excessive – but if you want to review a few weeks' training, it is surprisingly easy to use up the watch's lap memory.

Interval and countdown timers. If you can, buy a watch with two interval timers – this is especially useful for speedwork if you don't have access to a track. You can set one timer to countdown 3 minutes for a hard 800m, then the other for 90 seconds' recovery time. An alarm will sound every time you need to change pace, and you can usually record splits and total time as well.

Pacing alarm. Some top-end watches have an alarm that beeps to keep you on pace, which is especially useful if you are trying to work on your cadence.

Above: Few advanced runners train without a basic chronograph (or stopwatch) to time themselves.

Basics. Make sure your watch has a big, clear display – some are angled to make them easier to read when you are running; a durable strap; scratch-proof glass; a backlight for running in the dark; and is a good fit on your wrist (women may need to look for a female-specific watch, as men's watches may slip).

Heart-rate monitors

Once a tool for obsessives only, heart-rate monitors are now a fairly standard piece of kit for runners. Monitors range from a basic model that shows your heart rate and has a stopwatch, to top-end versions with 'virtual coaching'. Heart-rate monitors consist of a chest strap with electrodes (you need to wet these for the monitor to work well) and a transmitter, and a wrist unit, which picks up the signal and tells you your heart rate. Functions might include:

Left: The bigger and clearer your watch display, the more useful you will find it.

Left: Top-end GPS units use satellite data to measure your run and also monitor heart rate.

Below: This heart-rate monitor can be used to create detailed graphs of your performance data.

Above: Non-GPS speed and distance monitors use footpods like this one to give accurate measurements.

Left: Smaller units still offer a wide range of functions, the most basic being current heart rate.

with heart-rate data to give an estimate of how many calories you have burned during a session.

Heart-rate zones. You will be asked to set up heart-rate zones for different levels of activity (for example lower than 60 per cent of your maximum heart rate; 61 to 75 per cent; 76 to 90 per cent). The monitor then sounds an alarm to let you know how hard you are working, and you can use this to plan your interval training.

Calories burned. You can usually input personal details such as your weight and gender, and the monitor will combine this

Memory. Some monitors can store information about several workouts at once, including total time, splits, time in each pre-set heart-rate zone, average, minimum and maximum heart rate.

Software. Top-end models come with software for your home computer, which enables you to download and analyse information from your monitor, creating graphs and charts of your heart-rate data. This can be useful for evaluating and planning your training.

Speed and distance monitors

Often combined with a heart-rate monitor, speed and distance monitors (SDMs) fall into two categories. The less expensive models work with a footpod that attaches to your shoes, which sends information to the watch unit – you need to calibrate these models to get a more accurate reading, and they can lose accuracy on hills or uneven ground when your stride changes. The second type uses global positioning system (GPS) technology to give an accurate pinpoint of where you are and how fast and far you are running. The disadvantage with GPS-based monitors is that, in urban areas especially, you can lose contact with the satellite and be unable to take any measurements. SDMs usually come with the same features as a heart-rate monitor, but can combine this with data on your average speed, maximum and minimum speed, distance travelled, and sometimes cadence (on footpod models).

Left: They may be cumbersome, but GPS monitors are the easiest way for you to gauge your pace.

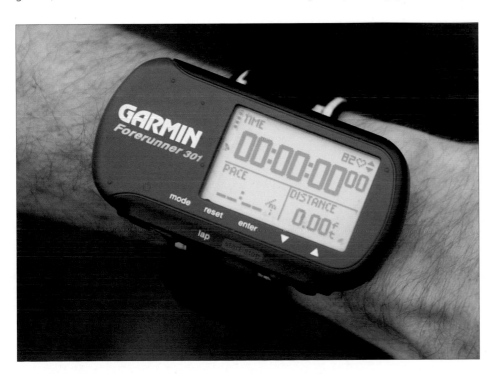

Periodization and Self-coaching

Great running performances always involve a little bit of luck. Weather conditions, catching a bug or tripping over could all spoil what would have been a perfect race. What really matters is the condition of the athlete on the day of the race.

The goal of runners at any level or distance is to be in their absolute peak condition – highly trained, but not overtrained – and that is the result of careful long-term planning or 'periodization'.

Track athletes almost always use periodization, as sprinting and middle-distance running have distinct seasons, but it is also a useful concept for long-distance runners, and one widely used by those at the top of the sport. The idea is to divide your training into different periods. First, the whole training year (sometimes called a macrocycle) is divided into broad phases lasting from a few weeks to a few months. Within this big picture are mesocycles of three to

Below: Dividing your training sessions into cycles ensures that you reach a peak when it comes time to race.

four weeks and microcycles of one or two weeks. Specific sessions don't need to be planned a year in advance, but the general theme is decided and, as you approach a particular period, specific days can be allocated to work on different areas of your training. The idea behind this planning is to allow your body to adapt to hard training, to bring yourself to a peak of fitness and speed in time for a particular race goal, and to recover and progress your training. Learning how to plan your own training year is essential if you are coaching yourself (as many recreational athletes do).

Successful self-coaching

A coach is a valuable asset for any runner (see box), but sometimes time and money mean we have to plan our own training. In this case,

Above: A training diary enables you to plan ahead and is a very valuable self-coaching tool.

you must learn to be as objective as possible about your running. A good coach will not simply hand you a training schedule. He will look at your lifestyle, how factors such as your career, family life or even your personality will affect the kind of training that is realistic for you. He will be able to listen to your problems and worries and adapt your training as necessary. If you are coaching yourself, you need to be aware of this and have the confidence to go with your instinct – for example if you have been feeling tired for weeks on end, recognize the need for a recovery week.

Planning, patience and progression

The secret to successful self coaching is the 'three Ps': planning, patience and progression. If you don't plan your training, you will become aimless and either do too much, too soon, or you will have the opposite problem and find that you never run any faster, which

Finding a coach

There is no doubt that any athlete will run better with than without a coach. The question is which coach, because working with someone who does not understand your needs is more likely to have a negative effect on your training.

A good coach should have an understanding of elite training – he may have been an international athlete himself – but should also be confident and happy coaching people at all levels and appreciating their individual limitations. When choosing a coach, remember that each one will have his own individual approach: some coaches favour lots of long, slow running; some believe in training with very high mileage; while others put an emphasis on cross-training. Make sure that you are happy with your coach's approach before you start training together.
If you are looking for a coach for the first time, a good place to start is your local running club, or the athletics governing body in your area.

saps your motivation. Lack of patience is the quickest route to injury and frustration. Any lack of progression in your training means you are unlikely to achieve your long-term goals.

If you are coaching yourself and are serious about improving your running, your training diary takes on a new level of importance, too. Instead of simply writing down your achievements at the end of each day, work out your training periods: when planning the year, write themes across the top of each week in

Above: It's vital to plan progressive training so that you continue to see improvements in your running.

pencil. Then map out your three to four-week cycles (for example, weeks one and two might be moderate, week three hard, week four easy) and your short-term goals. Plan your specific sessions a week or two in advance, so that you can be flexible and adapt your training if something isn't working (or working better than you expected!).

Planning your Training Year

Planning your training a long time in advance should, in theory, make your training easier and more successful. With a clear plan to follow you will be less tempted to throw yourself into last-minute training for a race or, on the other hand, to avoid stepping up your training.

The basic concept of periodization is built around the idea of training for a particular event, so before you plan your year, you will need to decide on your primary goal.

Setting a goal

For many distance runners the goal will be a marathon, which you can only race well once or twice a year;

Above: You can run short 'practice' races in your sharpening phase to fine-tune race speed.

if your goal is a shorter distance you may be able to race it several times over, but should aim to peak at a particular race. In order for periodized training to work well, you should choose a goal more than six months away so that you have time to build the foundation of your fitness (see below). Once you have chosen your goal race, you can work your planning backward from that date. You should also think about setting mini-goals – these might be shorter races (for example a half-marathon four to six weeks before a full marathon), or simply realistic time and distance targets for training.

Left: Before planning your training periods, you need to prioritize races for the coming year ahead.

Single and double periodization

If you have been running for several years, your body will have adapted to exercise and will not need such a long base phase. Some runners choose to have a double peak in their training year. This is normal for track and field runners, who want to peak for the indoor season in winter then the main season in summer; long-distance track runners might also aim to peak for the winter cross-country season. For road runners, especially those whose main event is the marathon, there are usually two peaks, in spring (March–April) and autumn (September–October). The training year might look like this:

January	Strength
February	Speed end/speed
March	Speed
April	Peak 1
May	Recovery
June	Base/strength
July	Speed endurance (inc. short races)
August	Speed
September	Speed
October	Peak 2
November	Recovery
December	Base

Training phases

Typical training phases over a year might be:

Base or foundation phase. There is no intense running during this phase. You are simply building up the number of miles you do slowly. The aim of this phase is to allow your body to make the physiological changes it needs to support the demands of more intense training: your muscles and tendons become stronger and your body becomes more efficient at transporting oxygen. The length of time spent in this phase is probably the most variable: a beginner or someone returning from injury could spend up to six months base building, while someone with many years of healthy running behind them could spend six to eight weeks in this phase.

Strength and conditioning phase. This is an important stage to go through to avoid injury and build the power of your muscles ready for faster running. You will maintain moderate mileage built up during your base phase, but start to add hill training, weight training and training on soft ground. Your stronger muscles will propel you forward faster, stabilize your joints and help alleviate fatigue in the late stages of a long race. You might spend one or two months in this phase.

Speed endurance phase. This phase can be incorporated into your strength phase, and experienced runners do some sort of speed endurance work all

Below: Running on soft ground during your strength and conditioning phase helps stabilize your joints.

year round. It is worth spending some time working on this area; think of it as a mini base-building phase for your shorter, quicker speedwork. During this period you will introduce threshold runs and long intervals once or twice a week, and you should spend anything from four to six weeks in this phase.

Speed or sharpening phase. This is when you bring all your preparations together, adding the leg speed that will make you a faster racer. You will add two or three faster speed sessions – ideally on a track – and reduce the amount of strength work you do, while maintaining a high mileage. During this phase you might also run some short races as a guide to your progress. This is the phase covered by most training schedules – the 8 to 16 weeks of true race preparation, and your goal race comes at the end of this period.

Recovery phase. Too often overlooked by runners, who may feel guilty about skipping training, this phase is crucial to racing well in your next training year. After your race, you might take a few days off running altogether, then ease back in with short, easy runs and cross-training.

Above: In the base or foundation phase, you'll work on building volume without intensity

Below: Your fastest speed sessions, on a track, will take place just before you complete your goal race.

Race Recovery

We have all heard stories about how hard elite runners train, but perhaps the most common mistake made by recreational athletes is thinking this means training as hard as you possibly can, as often as you can. Sometimes, not running is just as important.

Top athletes work just as hard at not running when necessary as they do at putting in 240km (150-mile) weeks. Missing out on essential recovery time will, at best, leave you exhausted and unable to run as fast as you would like; and at worst, ill or seriously injured. Taking easy weeks or weeks off should be part of your training on a cyclical basis (periodization), and it makes sense to put your longest recovery period after your hardest race of the year. There is a great deal of debate about the best way to recover from a race, but no doubt at all that it is necessary. Ideally, race recovery begins before you even reach the start line.

Before your race

The work you put in before a race, especially when that race is a marathon, is crucial to recovering well. If you have planned your training carefully and have had a long build-up with no interruptions from injury, then your muscles will be much better

Above: If weather conditions are tough on race day, you'll need to take longer to recover.

Below: In the weeks immediately before a race it's important to cut down on your training.

Above: When your training session hasn't gone to plan, sitting down and reconsidering your race goals will help.

prepared to cope with the demands of the race. Damage will be limited and recovery much quicker. It follows that if your training has not gone according to plan, you should revise your race goals to avoid placing undue stress on your body. Failure to do so leads to a downward spiral: your training goes badly, so the race goes badly, you skip recovery to get back into training and race better next time; then you become injured again and your next race is even worse. Treat your race as a high-quality training run, take some time out afterward and start from the beginning again.

The training you don't do is also very important. Before taking part in any race it is important to have a period of 'tapering', where you cut down your training to around 30 to 40 per cent of your highest workload for between one and three weeks

Left: Research has shown that the right nutrition and hydration before and during your race improves recovery time.

stress hormones that lower your immunity, and potentially causing damage to your undertrained muscles.

Nutrition is also essential to keep you well after the race. Countless studies have shown that marathon runners in particular report far higher than average rates of illness (usually colds) than the rest of the population (even athletes who have trained but do not complete a race). There are no definite explanations for this, but some studies have shown a link between carbohydrate consumption during the race (from sports drinks) and risk of illness afterward. One theory is that when your body switches to using fat for fuel, the stress hormone cortisol is released during the process; this blocks the actions of some immune responses. If you can keep your glycogen stores topped up throughout by drinking about one litre per hour of sports drink, then your body will not need to use as much fat for fuel, so less cortisol is released.

Below: Fit in extra time for rest and relaxation before you race, to reduce the impact of stress hormones.

before you race. The longer your goal distance, the more important the taper, so the week before a marathon you barely need to train at all. This taper period ensures your muscles have time to repair any minor damage from your intense training, and they can store enough fuel for your run. Some runners don't believe in tapering, but research has shown that runs of more than 16km (10 miles) two weeks or less before a marathon are detrimental.

Eating, drinking and sleeping well will also help your body meet its race demands. The female marathon world-record holder, Paula Radcliffe, eats around 3,000kcal (12,600kJ) per day and sleeps for 12 hours. You may not have time for 12 hours of sleep, but the principles that work for her will also work for you.

During the race

Try not to get carried away when you race. If you have put in the training, you should have an idea of the fastest pace you can realistically

aim for; stick to that. Running beyond your limits will ultimately lead to a poor race performance, which could take months to recover from psychologically. It also puts you at greater risk of injury and illness, raising your heart rate too high, releasing

After your Race

You may just feel like collapsing on the ground as soon as you finish a race, but try hard to resist the temptation. What you do in the first few minutes and hours afterward can have a real impact on your recovery.

When your race is finally over, however tempting it might be, don't stop moving. Walk around for at least 10 minutes immediately after finishing your race, staying tall and stretching out your arms and legs as you walk. This will help to keep your circulation up, starting the process of removing waste products that have built up (such as lactic acid). It is also a good way of gently stretching out your muscles – static stretching after a long, fast race is a bad idea, as your muscles will be riddled with tiny tears that could be worsened by intense stretching.

While you're walking around, start the process of refuelling your body with a light snack. It is not uncommon to feel nauseous after a race, but try to force some carbohydrates and protein down now and you will reap the benefits later. The ideal ratio for recovery is to eat 4g of carbohydrates for every 1g of protein, and recent

Above: Fight the urge to collapse after a race; have a gentle walk and try to refuel as quickly as possible.

research suggests that the protein will be used by the body more effectively if it is eaten immediately rather than a few hours later. The good news is that when your appetite returns later in the day, you can keep eating – you will have burned around 2,500kcal and used up 30 to 70g of protein during a marathon so you need to replenish those stores.

Reducing inflammation in your legs early on could also help with your recovery. You can take anti-inflammatory drugs to help with any aches and pains you have. Another (much-debated) treatment is ice baths, an idea popular with elite athletes. The obvious benefit is cooling and numbing your sore legs, and some say that the icing boosts circulation, again helping to remove

Mental recovery

Many athletes have a sense of anticlimax after taking part in a big race, and taking time off running can make matters worse. Try to use the time off positively – remind yourself that you worked hard for your race and deserve some time to yourself. You can use the time to refresh your training; review your training diary and analyse your performance in the race. Look at areas of your training that you think could be improved – perhaps if you had done more strength training, for example, you could have stayed more upright at the end of the race.

When you are training again, use the recovery period as a chance to try new activities or start work on an area of weakness, such as core strength. This will keep you feeling positive and give you a strong basis for your next training period.

waste products from the body. A massage might seem like a tempting prospect after 26.2 hard miles, but save it for a few days later – your legs will be too sore to be handled, and you risk causing further damage to your muscles.

Returning to running

Different athletes have very different approaches to returning to training after a race. Some jump straight back into speedwork, while others wait for weeks before pulling their trainers (sneakers) on again. The best path is somewhere between these extremes.

You might start to get itchy feet a few days after your race (especially if the result was good), but refrain from any running for a week after your race. At this stage there is no such thing as 'active rest' (cross-training to give your body a break); your muscles need to rest and refuel. After that, you can start to reintroduce gentle running and cross-training.

Below: Your body will cool down quickly after a race, so make sure that you wrap up warm.

Post-race problem-solving

Here are some of the most common post-race problems, and possible solutions

Problem	Before race	During race	After race
Muscle tears and sprains	Train well, taper well; work on strength and flexibility	Keep to your steady, pre-planned pace	Do not stretch; ice; rest
Colds	Taper	Take on 60–70g carbs per hour	Rest, sleep well, avoid sources of infection
Feeling down	Set realistic race goal, plan activities for the weeks after	Stick to your race plan and trust in it	Be proactive: analyse your race, then plan ahead
Poor, slow running	Taper	Keep to your planned pace; take on carbs	Eat carbs and protein; take a full weeks rest; sleep well

Treat the three or four weeks after your race as a reverse of your taper, starting at 30 to 40 per cent of your highest workload, and building back up slowly to what you would consider a full but light week of training. Avoid racing again until you are completely recovered – a good rule of thumb is to take a day off racing for every mile raced (so that is around a month off for a marathon).

Below: Some runners have a sense of anticlimax after their goal events, but planning ahead helps with this.

BRANCHING OUT

Running quickly becomes a way of life. That
doesn't mean that you should restrict yourself
to training on the track or road for the standard
distances; there is much more on offer if you want to
take your sport further. You can head off-road for
incredible views that can only be seen on foot; challenge
yourself by running a race that lasts five days; or try
your hand at multi-sport races. This chapter gives you a
general introduction to some of the ways you can
freshen up your running repertoire.

Above: As a general rule, the harder the run, the better the views!
Left: Mountain running is one way your fitness can take you to explore new heights.

Cross-country and Trail Running

Running off-road is very different experience to pounding out miles on the road. The exhilaration of coming back from a run, windswept, covered in mud and with lungs full of fresh air is matched only by the pain of slogging through miles of soggy ground.

Cross-country and trail running are at once closely related and miles apart. Both involve running through the countryside, often without markers, but the quick, fearless mindset of the cross-country racer could hardly be more different to the relaxed and enjoyment-focused approach of the trail runner.

Since both sports involve running on soft ground, they place special demands on your body. The impact on your joints is lessened, as the ground naturally absorbs more shock than the road, but the flip side is that your muscles have to work harder to push off, which can result in strained muscles and tendons in untrained off-roaders. Once you are used to the surface, however, it is an excellent form of training for all kinds of running, strengthening your legs (and your character) and improving your balance and core strength.

Below: Off-road running works on your balance and core strength but it takes a lot of practice.

Cross-country running
This has unpleasant associations for many of us: memories of being forced across muddy fields whatever the weather at school puts many people off trying again. However, cross-country races, which often form local leagues with fierce competition between clubs, are a great way to train fast and build strength

Above: Cross-country races often start much faster than road events and will help build your racing skills.

through the winter, in preparation for the next year's road and track seasons. Cross-country racing is notoriously fast and cut-throat, taking place over short distances (usually 5–9.5km/3–6 miles).

Proper preparation
Off-road running can strengthen your core muscles and improve your balance and proprioception (your spatial awareness and ability to negotiate uneven ground). However, if you go into trailing or cross-country after years of road running you will probably injure yourself before you feel any benefits, as these areas are so untrained. Before you go off-road for the first time, work on your core strength, and improve the balance and strength in your ankles using single-leg squats and wobble-board work – a coach or personal trainer will be able to show you how to use this.

Off-road kit

Try to run off-road in your usual trainers (sneakers) and you will soon be forced to give up. You need better grip and less cushioning on soft ground. Cross-country runners usually wear extremely light 'spikes' – slipper-like shoes with spikes in

the soles to claw through mud. Trail runners can choose from a huge range of shoes depending on the surface they intend to run on. For long-distance or fairly hard surfaces, bulkier trail shoes with cushioning are the best, while trail-racing shoes are closer to the cross-country model. The outer sole of the shoe should have deeper lugs for grip, the tongue should be gusseted to keep stones and water out, and the upper of the shoe may be waterproofed. Most trail shoes also include rock plates in the midsole to protect your feet from the hard ground and stones underfoot.

Left: Trail shoes have more protective outsoles than road shoes and are sometimes waterproof.

Above: There are not always distance markers in off-road races so you're racing others rather than the clock.

To stand a chance of running well, you must be prepared to go out fast from the gun – bottlenecks over stiles or through hedges are inevitable, and the farther forward you are the less these will delay you. To be successful you will need to develop a shorter, quicker stride than that for road running, striking the ground with your mid- or forefoot, since landing on your heel can make you sink into the ground or slip over. It can also be difficult to pace: there are usually no mile markers, so you are racing the other runners and not the clock – a skill that transfers well to road and track racing.

Trail running

As the name suggests, trail running is distinguished from other off-road running by the fact that it is run over public footpaths and marked trails. However, there is more to this type of running than waymarks. Trail races are usually more beginner friendly, and often take place over longer distances (some marathons and ultra-marathons are trail races). The ground, although soft, is usually slightly easier going as it is generally used for walking. The pace is easier going too – as

Right: Trail races are more relaxed than cross-country events and often offer beautiful surroundings.

in any race, the front runners are out to win, but this doesn't have the same fast start as a cross-country race. Overall times are inevitably slower than on the road, so you can relax and forget about your personal best.

Most people find that trail running is better for relaxing the mind than toughening it up. Races take place all year round, so if cold mud doesn't appeal, you can race on trails when summer is in full bloom and enjoy the scenery. Many coaches advise that all runners should do their long runs on trails wherever possible, because of the reduced impact on your joints and the distraction of the setting.

Mountain or Fell Running

If you've tried road running and off-road running, and have started to find that flat races are a little dull, or that your hill training sessions have started to feel easy, the only way is up. Literally – up a mountain.

The sport of mountain running (known as fell running in the UK) at its purest involves running up a mountain and back down the other side, though in the USA and continental Europe there's a great deal of crossover with trail races,

Below: In many mountain or fell races runners choose their own route, often over the most difficult ground.

so runners are more likely to keep to marked paths. Of course, fitness, strength and agility are all key attributes of mountain runners, but what really sets them apart is their courage: there is no time to apply the brakes as you hurtle down a 1,000m slope in a fell race.

The actual running involved in mountain races clearly needs to be very different to running on the flat

Above: Mountain running is not for the faint-hearted – here a fixed rope helps runners stay safe.

ground, or even on good trails. Even the best mountain runners accept that it's not usually possible to 'run' all the way up a mountain (fell races don't necessarily involve any scrambling or climbing, though the

Fell running categories

The Fell Running Association classifies fell races to show their difficulty:

Ascent	Category A	Minimum 76m (250ft) climb per 1.5km (1 mile); minimum 1.5km (1 mile) long; maximum 20% road
	Category B	Minimum 38m (125ft) climb per 1.5km (1 mile); max 30% on road
	Category C	Minimum 31m (100ft) climb per 1.5km (1 mile); max 40% on road
Distance	Category L	Long: minimum 19km (12 miles)
	Category M	Medium: minimum 9.5km (6 miles)
	Category S	Short: maximum 9.5km (6 miles)
Other	Category O	Orienteering-style race with checkpoints
	MM	Mountain Marathon

Rock of ages

In the UK, fell running originated in small, local races that were often part of fairs. The term fell is, strictly speaking, specific to the mountains and steep hills of the Lake District in Cumbria, north-west England, although it has been adopted in the UK to cover all mountain events. A popular challenge for fell runners now is to 'bag' as many Lake District peaks as possible inside 24 hours, the record being 77, while the classic test is the Bob Graham Round, a circuit of 42 peaks first completed by fell runner Graham in 1932.

In the USA, mountain running is a younger sport and is perhaps less visible thanks to the greater crossover with trail racing, but from the mid-90s onward the USA has had its own national mountain racing team, which competes internationally. In continental Europe and beyond, due in part to the different scale of the mountains, races tend to be longer and higher, with some held over a day or more (such as the annual Tour du Mont Blanc). These often follow paths and the routes are partly marked out, so they differ from British fell races. From these events, a new sub category called 'skyrunning' has emerged, which is basically long-distance events at high altitude.

Above: Even at the front of a mountain race it's rare to see people actually running up the ascents.

fastest runners might choose routes that do if they're the shortest). By the time they reach the top of the mountain, most will have slowed to a controlled climb. In training for fell races, runners need to build up their climbing muscles, using the kind of terrain and gradients expected in the race. However, the real skill comes on the descent, when the ability to allow yourself to 'fall' down the mountain comes into play. Quick feet, strong ankles and good balance and proprioception are essential if you are to get down in one piece. Near the top of mountains especially, there may be no trail, and the ground might consist of loose stones, so you need a light touch on the ground to avoid slipping. It goes without saying that the only way to get better

at mountain running is to practise running over mountains, but beginners should always keep safety in mind, training with an experienced mountain runner if possible, and starting with lower, gentler slopes.

Fell racing falls into a number of categories depending on steepness and distance. In its simplest form it bears some resemblance to cross-country running or orienteering: apart from the start and finish, the route is often unmarked and part of the skill of racing well is choosing the fastest route (which is rarely the easiest!). If it sounds scary, that's with good reason, as the remoteness of the route and added risk of injury from the steep, uneven ground can leave runners open to hypothermia if they become immobile. As such, fell runners

need to be able to navigate over mountainous ground, and have a basic knowledge of mountain safety. Though like all runners they dress as lightly as possible, they should carry basic safety kit such as a light layer of clothing to keep warm.

Below: Races are won and lost on the descent, with the most agile and fearless runners coming first.

Adventure Racing

As the name suggests, adventure racing is a sport for people who are tired of trudging around the block or obsessing over splits on the track. Adventure racing is an 'anything goes' multi-sport that gives you the chance to test yourself with new activities.

The fundamentals of adventure racing are off-road running and cycling, navigation, and often kayaking. Added to that list could be any number of physical and mental challenges: abseiling, ball games, archery, inline skating – whatever the organizers see fit to put you through. Adventure racers generally compete in mixed teams, and must complete the challenges while navigating around a set of check points as quickly as possible. Though often set in remote, rough countryside, some adventure races are staged in big cities: you may find yourself abseiling off a landmark building, or navigating through hidden alleys.

The beauty of adventure racing is that it is unpredictable and encourages you to take part in sports that you may never have considered. As such it is difficult to train for them too specifically. As a runner you will be at a clear advantage, since this and the bicycle are the main modes

Below: Adventure races can go on for days and some are deliberately staged at night for a dramatic atmosphere.

of transport between challenges. However, the surprise element of some races is such that it is more about having a go than becoming incredibly proficient at an activity. This, with the difficulty of navigation, means that surprise wins are not uncommon in adventure racing, where being fit and fast is not always the key to coming first.

Above: Don't expect an easy running route during adventure races – you'll need to get your feet dirty!

Developing team spirit

Unlike more standard running events, which are almost always individual pursuits, adventure racing is all about working together as a team. Ideally your team mates will have a good mix of skills so that you can help each other with your weakest tasks: one runner might do most of the map-reading, while a big, strong runner might carry more of the kit. Adventure racers sometimes use 'towing' to help less strong runners and cyclists: slower team members are literally 'towed' along using a bungee cord so they can go faster without tiring. If you are racing as a team, it is crucial that you stay together as there are usually penalty points for losing your team and reaching checkpoints separately.

Being part of a strong team is also crucial for the psychological side of adventure racing. Although

these events are designed to be fun – and they are – they can often go on for more than 24 hours, sometimes without any breaks for sleeping. You will need to be able to keep each other's spirits up when both your body and sense of humour inevitably start to fail.

Below: You won't know exactly what's in store until the race briefing, so be prepared to try anything.

Above: Team members must stick together to help each other both physically and mentally.

Benefits

If you do decide to give adventure racing a go, it can work wonders for your running when you return to normal events. It may not be suitable for those who want to win road races, but for the mid-pack runner, the different disciplines build your endurance, fitness and overall strength. Like triathlon, your risk of injury is lower because you tend not to use the same muscles in every training session, and your reduced running lowers the risk of impact-related injuries. Perhaps most importantly, taking part in one or two of these races each year gives you a mental break: since it is impossible to judge your performance against existing personal bests, you can enjoy instead the fitness you have built up through years of running.

Above: Kayaking is a regular feature of adventure racing so you'll need whole-body strength.

Navigation Basics

Anyone who spent their youth hiking and camping will be at a distinct advantage in off-road races. Map-reading is a skill that some people pick up very easily, but even if the idea frightens you, you can at least learn to find out where you are if you become lost.

The ability to run fast over difficult terrain is only part of off-road racing. All your training could go to waste if you lose hours on needless diversions caused by poor navigation. But it's not just about fast times: being able to find your way to the next checkpoint or the finish could be crucial for your safety.

Navigating fell races

A basic level of skill in navigation is essential for most adventure races and fell races (as well as orienteering events, which are entirely based around your ability to navigate). In fell races, navigation is secondary to running, as there are usually no checkpoints – you just have to get up and down a mountain as quickly as possible. Being able to use a map and compass simply enables you to find the quickest and safest route and to be able to get off the mountain if visibility becomes poor.

Above: Use the map to find out what kind of terrain you should be running on and use landmarks to stay on course.

Below: On adventure races you'll usually have to work in teams for safety.

Using a map and compass

Although it may sound daunting, in its simplest form, using a map and compass is straightforward. However, it is much easier to understand if you have a demonstration, and you can go on courses lasting a few hours to make you comfortable with the process. This is the basic procedure:

1 Holding your map as flat as possible, line up the edge of your compass with the direction in which you wish to travel (it doesn't matter which way you hold your map).

2 Turn the ring of your compass so that the guidelines are aligned with the north–south lines on the map. (N on the ring should be pointing north on the map.)

3 Hold the compass straight and flat in front of you and turn around until the north arrow is aligned with N on the compass ring. You are now facing in the direction you wish to travel.

4 Look in front of you for a feature that is marked on the map in your direction of travel (for example a boulder, building, or stream) and head toward it.

Left: Basic map-reading using a map and compass is a simple process.

Right: Once you've become a skilled navigator you will find that it is easier to cover courses much more quickly.

Navigating adventure races

In adventure racing your aim is much more complicated: you must visit as many plotted checkpoints as possible in the shortest time to win. Like fell races, there is no set route, so part of the skill is plotting a viable but direct route between checkpoints. You are given a dibber – an electronic tag – at the start of the race to record the checkpoints you have visited, and you will usually be given a map of the race area, as well as a detailed description of where the checkpoints are (giving grid reference and a description of the surroundings of each checkpoint).

In this type of race you will have to use your head constantly – there is no time to admire the beautiful scenery or you may find that you become lost. Help yourself by practising map-reading before your event using a standard walking map (the map you are given at the event will usually be a much larger scale, more detailed version). If at all possible, find out what kind of map you will be given at the event and practise using the same type, so that

Below: Clear running terrain may not always be easy to find – memorizing map symbols before your race will help.

you can learn the symbols for fences, streams, pits and other structural features, and how to determine the shape of the land. Unless you are in a very tough race, your checkpoint should be next to a feature, so you can find it with relative ease.

Plotting your course

At the start of your race, you should plot a course (by drawing on your map if possible) between checkpoints. Note which features you expect to pass on the way and where your significant changes of direction are. Before you reach each checkpoint,

know in which direction you will need to set out for the next one, as working it out at the checkpoint could help other teams find it, giving them an advantage. Most importantly, every time you set off again, look for a landmark or feature to check that you are going in the right direction – even after only a couple of minutes at the checkpoint you may become disoriented.

Of course, the safest way to approach your first navigational race is to run it as a team with a more experienced map-reader, who can show you the ropes as you go along.

Ultrarunning

If you thought marathon running was as much of a mental as a physical challenge, then ultrarunning is even more so. At 80km (50 miles) or more in length, ultra races are tough. But it's worth it – these can be some of the most dramatic, beautiful races in the world.

Although the idea of running farther than a marathon may seem daunting, if you have ever trained for this event you might be surprised by how little extra effort it takes to train for a 50K, 100-mile race or even a superhuman feat such as crossing the USA.

The ultrarunning scene has been dominated for a long time by slightly older runners – athletes whose natural speed is dropping off but whose endurance and mental strength are higher than ever. However, this is now changing and, as with all types of running, it is becoming more popular, as runners of all ages and abilities look for new challenges.

Going the distance

If you are still a competitive marathon runner you will need to put your usual running speed out of your mind. Patience is a virtue at these longer distances, and at 80km (50 miles) or more you can expect to add a couple of minutes per 1.5km (1 mile) to your usual marathon pace. That's

Below: Be prepared to run much slower than your usual race pace during longer ultrarunning events.

Above: Ultrarunning is tough but can take you to some of the most dramatic races in the world.

not to say the fastest ultrarunners in the world are slow – most would complete 50K faster than a fairly good runner could race a marathon – but unless you're at the very top, your aim will be completion rather than competition. Regular walk breaks are also a staple of ultrarunning strategy, even for sub-3-hour marathon runners. Typically you run for 15 to 20 minutes followed by a 3- to 5-minute walk break, taking care not to slump down or lose momentum.

Since your overall speed is slower during an ultramarathon, your speedwork is also longer and slower. You can forget about 400m repetitions on the track; your shortest intervals will be miles, run at around your half-marathon pace. If you are used to long threshold or tempo sessions, you will run those same longer intervals at your usual marathon race pace. In an ultra race, you will remain well below your lactate threshold unless you decide to run a sprint finish. If you have never carried out any strength training for shorter distances, then you should reconsider for ultra training. Spending hours on your feet often leads to a hunched posture and poor running style, which can eventually cause serious injuries. During an ultra race there is a greater need to carry more weight in the form of a fuel belt or backpack. Developing the muscles in your core, back and upper body will help you to stay strong and comfortable through the entire race.

Example schedule

Training for the beginners' ultra distance, 50K, is not that different to training for a marathon. The schedule below is a rough guide to how a 12-week plan could work. This assumes that you already have a base of fitness and have trained for a half or full marathon in the last year. Since this distance is only 8km (5 miles) longer than a marathon, the speed sessions are still fairly fast, although short intervals and leg-speed sessions are not included.

Right: It's crucial for ultrarunners to gain core strength to keep themselves in good form over the distance.

Ultrarunning schedule
(HMP = half-marathon pace)

	Mon	Tue	Wed	Thur	Fri	Sat	Sun
Week one	Rest	9.5km (6 miles) with 2 x 1.5km (1 mile) at 10K pace	8km (5 miles) easy	9.5km (6 miles) with 15 mins at HMP	Rest	9.5km (6 miles)	19km (12 miles)
Week two	Rest	9.5km (6 miles) with 3 x 1.5km (1 mile) at 10K pace	8km (5 miles) easy	9.5km (6 miles) with 20 mins at HMP	Rest	9.5km (6 miles)	22.5km (14 miles)
Week three	Rest	As week 2	2 x 5km (3 miles) easy (am/pm)	As week 2	Rest/6.5km (4 miles) easy	9.5km (6 miles)	25.5km (16 miles)
Week four	Rest	11km (7 miles) with 3 x 1.5km (1 mile) at 10K pace	2 x 6.5km (4 miles) easy	9.5km (6 miles) with 25 mins at HMP	Rest/6.5km (4 miles) easy	9.5km (6 miles)	29km (18 miles)
Week five	Rest	11km (7 miles) with 4 x 1.5km (1 mile) at 10K pace	2 x 6.5km (4 miles) easy	As week 4	Rest/6.5km (4 miles) easy	9.5km (6 miles)	32km (20 miles)
Week six	Rest	As week 5	1 x 5km (3 miles); 1 x 9.5km (6 miles)	11km (7 miles) with 30 mins at HMP	Rest/6.5km (4 miles) easy	13km (8 miles)	29km (18 miles)
Week seven	Rest	13km (8 miles) with 4 x 1.5km (1 mile) at 10K pace	1 x 5km (3 miles); 1 x 9.5km (6 miles)	As week 6	Rest/6.5km (4 miles) easy	13km (8 miles)	35km (22 miles)
Week eight	Rest	9.5km (6 miles) with 3 x 1.5km (1 mile) at 10K pace	8km (5 miles) easy	8km (5 miles) with 15 mins at HMP	Rest/6.5km (4 miles) easy	9.5km (6 miles)	22.5km (14 miles)
Week nine	Rest	As week 7	2 x 8km (5 miles) easy	11km (7 miles) with 30 mins at HMP	Rest/6.5km (4 miles) easy	13km (8 miles)	29km (18 miles)
Week ten	Rest	9.5km (6 miles) with 3 x 1.5km (1 mile) at 10K pace	2 x 6.5km (4 miles) easy	As week 9	Rest/6.5km (4 miles) easy	9.5km (6 miles)	25.5km (16 miles)
Week eleven	Rest	As week 10	9.5km (6 miles) easy	9.5km (6 miles) with 25 mins at HMP	Rest/6.5km (4 miles) easy	6.5km (4 miles)	19km (12 miles)
Week twelve	Rest	8km (5 miles) easy	Rest	8km (5 miles) easy	Rest	Rest	50K race

Ultrarunning: Longer Events and Stage Races

Once you begin to think about training for distances greater than 80km (50 miles), your training mileage to race distance ratio alters hugely. It is impossible to run this distance in a single training run, as your body would not be able to recover in time for your race.

When training for longer events, you have to push the mileage as high as you can, breaking the distance into manageable chunks, and have faith that on the day your mind will make up the rest. Despite this apparently impossible task, plenty of average people with busy lives find time to train for 100K races and beyond.

Long-distance training
To train for this kind of race, you can use the basic schedule from the previous page, but slow down your speed intervals further: for mile repetitions, use your half-marathon pace, and for the Thursday sessions use your normal marathon pace. You will also need to

Food supplies
In a normal road race you may rely on energy gels or drinks for food, but while these will play a big part in your ultra race, you obviously won't be able to live on them for hours or days on end. Experiment with different foods to see what your body can cope with. Remember that, as you are running quite slowly, digestion will be easier than during a marathon, but you may still find that you become nauseous after a long period of running.

Choose bland foods that are dense in calories, such as cold new potatoes, cheese sandwiches or plain potato crisps (chips). If your race is staged abroad, try to find out what food will be available and if it is unfamiliar, take some contingency supplies.

increase the mileage, which you can do in two ways: by increasing your Saturday run so that you do two long runs back to back, and by running twice most days. Obviously you will need to do this very slowly, so you can add another six to eight weeks building up mileage at the start of the training period.

Building up the distance
To build up your long runs, start with a run of around 9.5–13km (6–8 miles) on the Saturday (1 hour) and 16–19km (10–12 miles) on Sunday (90 minutes). Add 3km (2 miles) a week to the Sunday run until you reach 29km (18 miles), then gradually build up the Saturday run until both match. You can then take

Left: When training for races longer than 80km (50 miles) you should work toward having two long runs per week.

Above: Very long races and stage races can be gruelling, so work on your mental strategy beforehand.

Below: As you'll be increasing your mileage, you should try to run off-road more to reduce impact on your legs.

both runs up to 32km (20 miles). Don't exceed 3 hours running on either day, as your body will not be able to recover, and remember that your pace should be much slower than marathon race pace. Avoid any other activity (such as strenuous housework or gardening) on these days, and try to keep your runs off-road as much as possible to reduce the impact on your joints.

To run twice a day through the week, try using your run to commute to work (or part of the way). Some stage races require twice-a-day running, so this is good practice; while other stage races typically require 16–32km (10–20 miles) of running each day. Running to work also has the advantage that you will need to carry a backpack, which will help keep your pace down and teach you to run with extra weight if this is a feature of your race.

Mental preparation

You will know from your experiences racing shorter distances how powerful the mind can be in helping your running performance. While focusing on your race is the best approach for most shorter races, disassociation is definitely the best approach for the endless miles of an ultrarun. The race will be as much of an ordeal for your mind as your body, and you can expect at least two or three rough patches over a 100K race that will be bad enough to make you want to stop.

In a stage race, the second and third days are often the hardest, as you will have run hard but still have plenty to do. Expect these low points and prepare for them. If you can, take an MP3 player to pick you up, or join forces with a runner at a similar pace and chat (your slower pace allows you to do this). If all else fails, try repeating a mantra to yourself: 'I can do this', or 'I am strong and fit'.

Triathlon

If the growth of running as a mass participation sport has been rapid since the 1970s, the triathlon's emergence from relative obscurity has been astonishingly fast. Triathlons are races where competitors must swim, then cycle, then run.

Many runners change to triathlon because they have suffered impact injuries from high-volume running training; others simply enjoy the new challenge. It is certainly a good way to build all-over fitness, and you may find that your running times improve as a result of the more varied training.

Although the three sports of swimming, cycling and running have been combined for years, the modern sport of triathlon is widely accepted to have started in California in the 1970s, created

Below: Swimming with hundreds of other people is one of the skills you need to master for triathlon.

by friends who trained together in the different disciplines and decided to hold a race. The first event, the Mission Bay Triathlon in San Diego, California, was held in 1974. A few years later, the first Ironman or full-distance triathlon was held in Hawaii, following a debate between runners, swimmers and cyclists over who had the greater endurance fitness. Three races already in existence on the island – the 4km (2.4-mile) Waikiki Roughwater Swim, 185km (115-mile) Around Oahu Bike Race and the Honolulu marathon – were combined, with 5km (3 miles) taken off the bike course to create a continuous route. Only 15 athletes took part, but the Ironman distance – now held all

Above: The right kit can help you to achieve faster times in triathlon, especially during the cycling phase.

over the world, with championships in Hawaii – now attracts tens of thousands of runners every year. A shorter triathlon became an Olympic event in 2000 and, although the sport is still young, there are now athletes specializing in this combination sport.

Don't be fooled into thinking that because you are a good runner, you will make a good triathlete. Everyone can ride a bike, but racing on one is a different skill, while few adults are good swimmers. Even if you have some background in these sports, you will need to change your approach and technique to ensure a comfortable transition from one to the next. Swimming, cycling and running in triathlon are geared toward moving as quickly as possible with the least amount of energy expenditure, with minimum upset when switching from one set of muscles to the next. The time taken to change kit between each stage (called transition – the first change is T1, the second T2) is also recorded to give the final time. Triathlon kit is geared toward making this process as smooth as possible.

Standard triathlon distances			
	Swim	**Bike**	**Run**
Super sprint	400m	10K	2.5K
Sprint	750m	20K	5K
Olympic/Short	1,500m	40K	10K
Middle/Half Ironman	1.9K (1.2 miles)	90K (56 miles)	21K (13.1 miles)
Long/Full Ironman	3.8K (2.4 miles)	180K (112 miles)	42k (26.2 miles)

Above: Transition – where triathletes change from one discipline to the next – is sometimes known as 'the fourth discipline of triathlon'.

All the gear

If you like running for its simplicity and lack of expense then triathlon, along with adventure racing, is probably not for you. Race entry is two or three times that of a running race, but the real cost is the kit needed to train and compete. If you are trying out triathlon, consider buying some kit (such as the bike) second hand, or look out for triathlon packages from specialist shops. Your biggest purchases will be:

Triathlon suit. An all-in-one or two-piece technical suit, designed to be worn through the whole race to avoid the need for changing. It is quick drying, and has padding for the cycle stage.

Wetsuit. Most triathlons involve an open-water swim, and wetsuits are often required. A wetsuit will keep you warm and help with buoyancy.

Bike. You don't need to spend a fortune on a bike, but the more you pay, the lighter and more efficient your bike will be. Triathlon-specific bikes have a different fit to traditional road bikes to preserve your running muscles and aid efficiency. They are often fitted with tri bars or aerobars, which enable you to lean forward with your forearms pointing ahead, making you more aerodynamic.

Bike shoes and pedals. Special clipless pedals with corresponding shoes allow your feet to clip on to the pedals, so you can pull them up as well as pushing down, generating more power.

Triathlon shoes. Of course, you can use your standard running shoes, but triathlon shoes are lighter, dry quicker, and are easier to pull on and fasten.

Left: Wetsuits are often compulsory in open-water swims.

Right: Special lightweight triathlon shoes help you make the most of your strongest discipline.

Triathlon: Training Sessions

For many runners, coming to triathlon after years of focusing on putting in running miles, swimming and cycling are distant childhood memories. Consequently the runner either dreads getting back into the pool or on the bike, or remembers these sports as simple fun.

Cycling and swimming are fun, but they're certainly not simple. You will need to go right back to basics in order to learn how to swim and cycle effectively, and more importantly, how to combine them with your 'first' sport.

Swimming

Freestyle (front crawl) is by far the most commonly used stroke in triathlon, but it is difficult to get right. You need to achieve as efficient a stroke as possible to conserve energy for the later stages of the race, while at the same time learning how to 'sight' (raise your head to check you are on course), and survive the rough-and-tumble of the triathlon swim. Triathletes aim to use their legs less than usual in the swim, to save the muscles for the bike and run sections, but you will need to practise kicking harder toward the end of your swim to force blood into the muscles you are about to use.

If it has been years since you swam, or you never learned, attending adult classes will be useful. There are four basic components to good freestyle stroke:

Body position. You should be lying horizontally at the top of the water, face down; your feet should break the surface when you kick without bending excessively at the knee.

Breathing. Learn to breathe on both sides. Most people find it easiest to breathe every third stroke. Don't lift your head, but turn with the motion of your body as your arm comes out of the water.

Kick. Move your legs from the hip, toes pointed and feet close together, and without bending your knees too much.

Stroke. Reach ahead of you and curve your hand to 'catch' the water. Pull right through, keeping your arm straight through the stroke, past your hip, and only bending the elbow to return the arm to the front.

Swim sessions:

Sets. Use sets of ten laps of the pool with rests in between, first to build up your endurance, then to do speed intervals as you become more confident.

Above: Taking swimming lessons will make you more efficient in the water, saving energy for the bike and run stages.

Below: You'll need to kick harder at the end of the swim so you're ready to stand, run and cycle.

constant, and practising taking on sports drinks as you go, since in a triathlon this will be your best opportunity to do so.

Hills. Try hill sprints or longer drags to build power in your legs, but remember to keep your action smooth and steady – if your pedalling slows right down, change gear.

Spinning. Triathletes use easy 'spinning' on an easy gear to help flush lactic acid out of their legs and prepare for the run section of the race. Try a few minutes of this at the end of your rides.

Running
If you decide to commit to triathlon training, you will need to cut down to three or four runs per week, and your long run probably won't be as long as you are used to. All of your run sessions are quality sessions, however, so you might do a speedwork session, threshold run, long run and a triathlon-specific session called a brick. This involves alternating cycling and running and is more easily done in the gym. The idea is to become used to the sensation of running after cycling, when the blood will have pooled in your cycling muscles and will take time to shift to your running muscles.

Below: This hands-on-top steering position helps beginners to feel in control – and elite triathletes to climb hills.

Above: Use bike/run 'brick' sessions to get used to running fast straight after a period of cycling.

Stroke count. Count the number of strokes you use to swim one lap. Aim to reduce the number of strokes.

Catch ups. This works on your stroke. Instead of moving your arms continuously, keep your right arm out in front of you until the left arm meets it, then as soon as your hands are side by side, stroke with your right arm, and so on.

Cycling
You may not be used to using a road bike, so take time to get used to the fast feel and more responsive steering. If you

are using clipless pedals for the first time, practise in a traffic-free area first. When you buy your bike, get fitted in a specialist shop – this could save hours of agony later on, or at the very least make you a more efficient cyclist. When you are starting out, hold the handlebars at the front, on top of the brakes, so that you can use them if necessary; when you are ready, start using the 'drops' (the underneath, curved part of the handlebars). Invest in a cycle computer so that you can monitor your cadence.

Bike sessions:
Long rides. Endurance cycling needs hours of training, so include one long ride in your training each week, learning to use the gears to keep your effort

Triathlon: Olympic Distance Training

Running makes you incredibly fit. There is no doubt about that, but if you have been feeling smug about your improved athleticism, you may be in for a shock when you start triathlon training, which involves a much higher level of overall fitness.

Aside from the technical difficulty of learning new sports, triathlon requires a level of whole-body strength and fitness that running, with its very specific gains, does not. If you are new to triathlon, Olympic distance (1,500m/40K/10K) is a good place to start: it is not so long as to wear you out with high-volume training, but long enough to test out your new-found swimming and cycling skills.

Fitness levels

As with any race you will need a base of fitness. If you have not been swimming or cycling for a few years, spend two or three months building them into your training schedules, starting with just one swim and bike ride a week. You will also need to cut down the number of runs you do, since you will be

Above: Even after reducing training sessions for triathlon, running is likely to remain your strongest discipline.

Left: Don't jump straight into a triathlon training plan as you'll need to build up your cycling and swimming fitness first.

Finish times

If you are new to competing in triathlons it is difficult to know what kind of finish times you can expect.

At the fast end of an Olympic distance race, male competitors will finish in under 1hr 45 mins (<20 mins swim; <2 mins T1; <55 mins bike; <30 secs T2; <33 mins run). Top female athletes complete in well under 2 hours in total. For an average competitor, a sub-2:30 time is considered fast, while anything below 3 hours is a very decent effort.

Triathlon: beginners' 10-week schedule

	Mon	Tue	Wed	Thur	Fri	Sat	Sun
Week one	Swim: 10 WU; 2 x 10 fast; 10 CD	Run: 4 miles easy	Cycle: 1hr easy	Swim: 40 easy	Rest	Brick: 3 x 15 mins bike, 5 mins run	Run: 1hr, 9.5–13km (6–8 miles) easy
Week two	Swim: 10 WU; 10 SC; 10 CD	Cycle: 1hr with 2 x 10 mins faster	Run: 8km (5 miles) easy	Swim: 40 with 10 CU	Run: 6.5km (4 miles) with 4 x 2 mins fast	Rest	Brick: 45 mins bike, 30 mins run
Week three	Cycle: 1hr over hills, using gears	Swim: 10 WU, 2 x 10 fast; 10 CD	Run: 8km (5 miles) with 4 x 2 mins fast	Swim: 50 easy	Rest	Run: 1hr15	Brick: 4 x 10 mins bike, 5 mins run
Week four	Swim: 30 easy	Cycle: 45 mins flat and fast	Rest	Run: 8km (5 miles) with 15 mins threshold	Rest	Cycle: 1hr easy	Run: 1hr easy
Week five	Swim: 10 WU; 10 CU; 2 x 8 fast; 10 CD	Brick: 5 x 10 mins bike, 5 mins run	Run: 8km (5 miles) easy	Swim: 50 easy	Rest	Run: 1hr30 16–7.5km (10–12 miles)	Bike: 1hr20 with steady hills
Week six	Swim: 60 easy	Run: 10 mins warm-up, 3 x 1.5km (1 mile) at 10K pace; cool-down	Bike: 1hr easy	Swim: 10 WU; 500m timed; 10 CD	Rest	Bike: 1hr45 steady	Run: 1hr30
Week seven	Swim: 10 WU; 10 SC; 10 fast; 10 SC; 10 CD	Brick: 4 x 15 bike, 5 run	Run: 8km (5 miles) with 3 x 1.5km (1 mile) at 10K pace	Swim: 50 with 20 faster	Rest	Run: 1hr with 6 x 2 mins faster	Bike: 1hr on hills using gears
Week eight	Swim: 10 WU; 10 SC; 300m fast; 10 CD	Run: 9.5km (6 miles) with 6 x 3 mins fast, 2 mins easy	Bike: 1hr15 mins steady	Swim: 10 WU; 3 x 8 fast; 10 CD	Rest	Run: 1hr15 easy	Swim: 500m, change, bike: 45 mins; run 20 mins
Week nine	Rest	Swim: 10 WU; 500m timed;10 CD	Run: 8km (5 miles) easy	Bike: 16–24km (10–15 miles) flat, timed	Swim: 60	Rest	Bricks: 3 x 10 mins bike, 5 mins easy
Week ten	Rest	Swim: 40 easy	Run: 6.5km (4 miles) easy	Bike: 45 mins steady	Rest	Bricks: 2 x 10 bike, 5 run, easy	Triathlon

Swim sessions: CU = catch-ups; SC = stroke count; WU = warm-up; CD = cool-down. Figures represent 25m laps.

unable to fit in more than three runs a week once you start triathlon training. Work on your weakest discipline most to build up your confidence.

Keeping records

Your training diary will be more important than ever when you start triathlon training, as the training is much more complex and you will probably do more sessions per week than with straight running training. This will help you to make sure you are doing enough in each discipline, and to chart your progress in your less familiar sports.

Right: Practising swim drills will improve your stroke and gradually help you to speed up in the water.

Taking Your Running Further: Destination Events

Combining your love for running and the hard-won fitness it has brought with a trip to an exotic location is the perfect way to see more of the world. Here are some of the most spectacular must-do events for runners of all abilities.

Himalayan 100 Mile Stage Race, Darjeeling, Mirik, India

The best race in the world for a true runner's high, this 'undulating' five-day race is tough, but perfectly accessible. Every October, in stages ranging from 16–48km (10–30 miles), although officially the longest stage is marathon distance, about 100 runners climb and drop thousands of feet at altitudes between 1,980m–3,600m (6,500ft–11,800ft). Starting in Darjeeling, they run over rough tracks, past tea plantations and pine forests and through remote villages, where the welcome is always warm. It is a difficult race, but with marathon-level fitness you should be able to complete it – and it will be worth the hardship for the race's main selling point: stunning panoramic views of four of the world's five highest peaks, including Mount Everest. www.himalayan.com

Right: Mount Kanchenjunga watches over runners on day two of the Himalayan Stage Race.

Below: Running at altitude for five days is tough, but there is a huge support team on hand and, of course, constantly stunning views.

Hood to Coast Relay, Oregon, USA

If you find running to be a lonely sport, then this race is for you. It's the world's biggest relay, running 315km (197 miles) from the awe-inspiring Mount Hood to the Pacific coast in Oregon – home to one of world's biggest running shoe manufacturers, Nike, and to American running legend Steve Prefontaine. The race began in 1982 with just 8 teams, and now every year in August 1,000 teams of 12 make the journey with the slower teams starting out first. There are 36 legs ranging from just over 6km (3½ miles) to just under 13km (8 miles) and to take part, and you need to average a pace of about 14 minutes per kilometre. But don't think this race is about running fast: the emphasis is on fun and teamwork, with competitions for best decorated vans (teams are allowed two each to carry all their supplies) and best team names. Teams work together to support each other, handing out food, drink and moral support to fellow members along the way. If you would like to be one of them next year, you will need to be quick off the mark: the race tends to sell out in a day. www.hoodtocoast.com

Above: The spectacular Mount Hood provides an impressive backdrop to the start of the Hood to Coast Relay.

Below: Competitors cross the start line as they prepare to complete a distance of 315km (197 miles) in 36 stages.

Boston Marathon, Boston, USA

This historic marathon in a historic city is one that every runner should aim to add to their list, for one simple reason: Boston Marathon has strict qualifying times for entry, which means that running it puts you firmly in the faster than average category. In fact, those times are not too intimidating: 3:10 for men and 3:40 for women, slowing down with age category. Apart from the prestige of gaining an entry, runners enjoy the sense of tradition. The marathon started in 1897, making it the oldest annually held marathon in the world. Like the city's history, it has not been without conflict: in 1967, before the Amateur Athletic Union allowed women to run in long-distance events, Kathrine Switzer entered the race without giving her gender. Officials tried to remove her from the course, but other runners surrounded her so that she could finish. These days, more than 20,000 entrants of both sexes enjoy the slightly downhill, point-to-point run, finishing in Boston's Copley Square. www.bostonmarathon.org

Above: Officials try to remove Kathrine Switzer from the Boston Marathon in 1967; women are now very welcome!

Below: The race's entry conditions help ensure its popularity, as qualifying marks you out as a 'real' runner.

Above: The relentless icy white of the landscape provides a unique backdrop to the race.

Left: You can't be overdressed for this race – snow shoes are essential.

Below: Competitors in the North Pole Marathon run laps of a temporary camp on the shifting ice.

North Pole Marathon, Arctic Circle

If crowded big-city marathons are not for you, then this relatively new race could be the answer. Running on sea ice near the North Pole, there is not actually much to look at: you will run laps of a temporary camp on the ice, but sheets of white stretching into the distance give the event a surreal and unique atmosphere. Naturally, there is no need to worry about overheating, but participants should consider revising their usual personal bests, since the addition of snow shoes, layers of clothing and temperatures well below freezing can slow you down considerably. Running is all about seeing different places, and this is certainly one of the more unusual.

www.npmarathon.com

Sun Herald City to Surf, Sydney, Australia

For a race that feels more like a giant street party, you can't do better than this 14K event, held in August. Said to have been inspired by San Francisco's Bay to Breakers event, it began in 1971 with a respectable 2,000 competitors. It has gone on to become one of the biggest road races in the world with more than 63,000 finishers in 2006. Starting in the city's Hyde Park and running down to the famous Bondi Beach, it is one of the friendliest, liveliest races on the planet, full of costumes and characters. For most of the people who participate in City to Surf, the finishing time is not important, but the lead runners still complete the race in little more than 40 minutes.
http://city2surf.sunherald.com.au

Left: Tens of thousands of runners crowd the streets of Sydney in one of the world's biggest road races.

Below: The emphasis of the City to Surf, for most of the participants, is on fun and celebration.

Above: Competitors in the Great Wall Marathon wind their way through the beautiful Tianjin Province.

The Great Wall Marathon, Tianjin Province, China

Marathons are rarely much tougher, nor the rewards more spectacular, than this annual run along the Great Wall of China, which takes place in May. Participants must conquer the winding stone course, which includes many steep ascents and descents, as well as over 5,000 stone steps. Race organizers suggest that one of the best ways of preparing for this marathon is to run up and down the stairs of a 20-storey building! Aside from the main marathon, a half-marathon, 10K and 5K runs are also held each year. This is a popular event: in 2008 over 1,700 runners conquered the Wall over the four different distances. Competitors are treated to breathtaking views of the surrounding Tianjin Province as they explore one of the world's most famous landmarks in this truly unique event.
www.great-wall-marathon.com

Above: Though without doubt an arduous climb, the views along this course are spectacular.

Below: Exhausted runners literally crawl up some of the 5,000-plus stone steps which form part of the course.

Marathon des Sables, Morocco

This six-day event, which started in 1986 and is held in April, is billed as the toughest foot race on earth for good reason. Drawn by the other-worldly beauty of the Moroccan sand-dunes and the lure of the challenge, most competitors come to regret entering this event at some point while running through 225km (150 miles) of heat and sand, which includes a single stage of 78km (52 miles). Runners have to carry all their own belongings (the organizers supply water and tents) throughout the race. Medical attention for dehydration and ruined feet is in high demand. However, it is the formidable reputation of this event, and the satisfaction and experience of completing it, that keeps it selling out more than a year in advance every time.
www.darbaroud.com

Right: Over 15km of plaster (Band-Aid) is used in every Marathon des Sables race.

Below: Competitors must carry all their own kit for the whole 225km (150 miles).

Above: A suitably dressed runner in the Marathon du Medoc crosses through Pauillac vineyards.

Below: Spectators look on as a competitor samples some of the local wine on offer around the course.

Marathon du Medoc, Pauillac, France

It is difficult to imagine a greater contrast to the arduous Marathon des Sables than the Marathon du Medoc, run in September each year, even though it sells out almost as quickly.

Bizarrely, the main attraction at this marathon is not the glorious countryside scenery, the jolly atmosphere or the slick organization; it is the aid stations. However, these are no ordinary tables laid out with sorry half-full cups of water or energy drinks. This unique race runs through France's most famous wine-producing region and samples of local wine are on offer at 21 different stops through the race, along with other fuels ranging from freshly baked French bread to delicacies such as foie gras and oysters. Fast times are more than possible on this course, but to attempt one really is to miss the point of the event.
www.marathondumedoc.com

Monaco Marathon, Monte-Carlo, Monaco

Established in 1997, this unique marathon takes its 3,000-plus competitors through three different countries, as Monaco itself is too small to host the whole distance. The route starts in Monte-Carlo, follows the coast into France and then Italy before it turns back, taking competitors back through France again, finally finishing with a lap around Monaco's Louis II Stadium.

Runners are given a special 'marathon passport' which they must get stamped in each country. With its glamorous location, spectacular views of the Côte d'Azur, and almost guaranteed sunshine, it is not hard to see why this race becomes more and more popular each year.
www.monaco-marathon.com

Right: Competitors run through the famous harbour in Monte-Carlo before crossing the border into France then Italy.

Below: Runners can expect clear weather and wonderful views of the stunning Côte d'Azur.

Old Mutual Two Oceans Marathon, Cape Town, South Africa

Calling itself 'the world's most beautiful race', the Two Oceans Marathon is a 56km (35 mile) ultramarathon held annually in Cape Town, South Africa, on the Saturday of the Easter weekend.

The race begins in Newlands, and follows a circular route through Muizenberg, Fish Hoek, over Chapman's Peak and Constantia Nek, and eventually finishes at the University of Cape Town campus. The route covers open road and more challenging mountain climbs, with stunning views of both the Indian and Atlantic oceans, the two oceans that give the race its name.

A popular half-marathon, which has become the biggest in South Africa, is also held on the same day as the ultramarathon.
www.twooceansmarathon.org.za/

Below: Competitors race on open road before tackling the more difficult mountain climbs.

Above: The race is run against a backdrop of spectacular scenery through the Cape Peninsula.

Resources

Books

Austin, Michael, *Running and Philosophy: A Marathon for the Mind*, Blackwell, 2007

Bean, Anita, *The Complete Guide To Sports Nutrition*, A&C Black, 5th edition, 2006

Bingham, John, *No Need for Speed: A Beginner's Guide to the World of Running*, Rodale, 2004

Burfoot, Amby, *The Runner's World Complete Book of Running for Beginners*, Rodale, 2005

Daniels, Jack, *Daniels' Running Formula*, Human Kinetics, 2nd edn, 2004

Dick, Frank W., *Sports Training Principles*, A&C Black, 4th edn, 2002

Fee, Earl, *The Complete Guide to Running: How to be a Champion from 9 to 90*, Meyer & Meyer Sports Books, 2005

Fitzgerald, Matt, *Brain Training for Runners*, New American Library, 2007

Hamlett, Alison, *Need to Know? Running*, Collins, 2007

Jackson, Lisa & Whalley, Susie, *Running Made Easy*, Anova, 2nd edn, 2008

Kowalchik, Claire, *The Complete Book of Running for Women*, Simon & Schuster, 2000

McConnell, Kym, and Horsley, Dave, *Extreme Running*, Pavilion Books, 2007

Noakes, Tim, *The Lore of Running*, Human Kinetics, 2002

Smith, Mike, *High Performance Sprinting*, Crowood Press Ltd, 2005

Websites

www.runnersworld.com
www.runnersworld.co.uk
www.runningtimes.com
www.mapmyrun.com
www.marathonguide.com
www.aimsworldrunning.org

Metric/imperial conversions for popular race distances

Race distance	Conversion
100m	109.3 yards
1km	0.62 miles
1 mile	1.6 km
1,500m	1,640.4 yards
5K	3.1 miles
10K	6.2 miles
10 miles	16.1 km
Half-marathon	13.1 miles/21.1 km
Marathon	26.2 miles/42.2km

Useful Contacts

American Running Association
4405 East-West Highway
Suite 405, Bethesda, MD 20814
USA
www.americanrunning.org

Berlin Marathon
Sport-Club Charlottenburg e.V.
Glockenturmstr. 23
14055 Berlin, Germany
www.berlin-marathon.com

European Athletic Association (EAA)
Avenue Ruchonnet 18
Lausanne, CH 1003, Switzerland
www.european-athletics.org

International Association of Athletics Federations (IAAF)
17 Rue Princesse Florestine
BP 359, MC98007 Monaco
www.iaaf.org

Komen Race for the Cure
5005 LBJ Freeway, Suite 250
Dallas, TX 75244, USA
www.raceforthecure.com

London Marathon
115 Southwark Street
London SE1 0JF, UK
www.london-marathon.co.uk

New York City Marathon
9 East 89th Street
New York, NY 10128, USA
www.ingnewyorkcitymarathon.org

Paris Marathon
A.S.O. Athlétisme
2 Rue Rouget de Lisle, TSA 61100
92137 Issy-les-Moulineaux Cedex
France
www.parismarathon.com

Race for Life
Cancer Research UK
61 Lincoln's Inn Fields
London WC2A 3PX, UK
www.raceforlife.org

Road Runners Club of America
1501 Lee Hwy, Suite 140
Arlington, Va. 22209, USA
www.rrca.org

UK Athletics
Athletics House
Central Boulevard, Blythe Valley Park
Solihull B90 8AJ, UK
www.ukathletics.net

USA Track & Field (USATF)
132 East Washington Street
Suite 800
Indianapolis, USA
www.usatf.org

World Association of Veteran Athletes
www.world-masters-athletics.org

Race time predictor

Use a recent race performance to predict your finish time over another distance. The closer the two distances, the more accurate the prediction will be.

Mile	5K	10K	Half-marathon	Marathon
4:00	13:18	27:43	1:01:05	2:07:21
4:10	13:51	28:52	1:03:37	2:12:38
4:20	14:24	30:01	1:06:09	2:17:55
4:30	14:58	31:12	1:08:46	2:23:22
4:40	15:31	32:21	1:11:18	2:28:39
4:50	16:04	33:29	1:13:48	2:33:52
5:00	16:37	34:38	1:16:20	2:39:08
5:10	17:11	35:49	1:18:56	2:44:34
5:20	17:44	36:58	1:21:28	2:49:51
5:30	18:17	38:07	1:24:01	2:55:10
5:40	18:50	39:15	1:26:30	3:00:20
5:50	19:24	40:26	1:29:07	3:05:48
6:00	19:57	41:35	1:31:39	3:11:05
6:10	20:30	42:44	1:34:11	3:16:21`
6:20	21:03	43:53	1:36:43	3:21:38
6:30	21:37	45:04	1:39:20	3:27:06
6:40	22:10	46:12	1:41:50	3:32:18
6:50	22:43	47:21	1:44:22	3:37:35
7:00	23:17	48:32	1:46:58	3:43:01
7:10	23:50	49:41	1:49:30	3:48:18
7:20	24:23	50:50	1:52:02	3:53:34
7:30	24:56	51:59	1:54:34	3:58:51
7:40	25:30	53:09	1:56:09	4:02:09
7:50	26:03	54:18	1:59:41	4:09:31
8:00	26:36	55:27	2:02:13	4:14:48
8:10	27:09	56:36	2:04:45	4:20:05
8:20	27:43	57:47	2:07:22	4:25:33
8:30	28:16	58:56	2:09:54	4:30:49
8:40	28:49	1:00:04	2:12:34	4:36:23
8:50	29:22	1:01:13	2:14:56	4:41:19
9:00	29:56	1:02:24	2:17:32	4:46:44
9:10	30:29	1:03:33	2:20:04	4:52:01
9:20	31:02	1:04:42	2:22:36	4:57:18
9:30	31:35	1:05:50	2:25:06	5:02:31
9:40	32:09	1:07:01	2:27:43	5:07:58
9:50	32:42	1:08:10	2:30:15	5:13:15
10:00	33:15	1:09:19	2:32:47	5:18:32

Index